This book is presented to

_____

from

_____

on this date

_____

Published by B&H Publishing Group, Nashville, Tennessee
Hand-lettering: Kristi Smith–Juicebox Designs
Dewey Decimal Classification: J220.95
Subject Heading: GOD—PROMISES / BIBLE STORIES

Scripture quotations are taken from The Christian Standard Bible.
Copyright © 2017 by Holman Bible Publishers. Used by permission.
Christian Standard Bible®, and CSB® are federally registered trademarks
of Holman Bible Publishers, all rights reserved. Scriptures are also taken
from The Holy Bible, English Standard Version. Copyright © 2001 by
Crossway Bibles, a publishing ministry of Good News Publishers.

Printed in April 2020 in Shenzhen, Guangdong, China
3 4 5 6 7 8 9 • 24 23 22 21 20

THE
PROMISES OF GOD
STORYBOOK BIBLE

THE STORY
OF GOD'S
UNSTOPPABLE
LOVE

BY JENNIFER LYELL

ILLUSTRATED BY THANOS TSILIS

B&H
kids

Nashville TN

Words of Affirmation

"As the parent of a child who was taught the Bible in Sunday School by Jennifer Lyell, I am amazed by the vitality, energy, and imagination she brings to that ancient calling. In this beautiful book, Jennifer takes children and grown-ups to the Bible with both truth and beauty. *The Promises of God Storybook Bible* will prepare children to engage with the Bible for the rest of their lives. Children will love this book and will ask for it to be read over and over again. More importantly, this book will help them to love the Bible itself, and to hide its truths in their hearts."

—**RUSSELL MOORE**, *PRESIDENT, THE ETHICS & RELIGIOUS LIBERTY COMMISSION OF THE SOUTHERN BAPTIST CONVENTION*

"The seeds of Scripture were planted in my heart from my earliest childhood, and I began following Christ at the age of four. So I know firsthand that God moves in the hearts of children to draw them to Himself. For years I have observed Jennifer Lyell live this conviction out by teaching the Bible to pre-schoolers in her church. The conviction that little ones can learn big Truth motivates Jennifer and is at the heart of *The Promises of God Storybook Bible.* With stories drawn from the biblical text and crafted to capture the attention of young hearts, this book will help your child come to know and trust the God of the Bible. As you read it to or with your child, your own heart will be encouraged by the faithfulness of our God who always keeps His promises."

—**NANCY DEMOSS WOLGEMUTH**, *AUTHOR; FOUNDER/TEACHER OF REVIVE OUR HEARTS*

Dedication

*With love and gratitude to the children and families
of Grace Community Church of Nashville
for all you have shown me of the promises of God.*

*And in loving memory and honor of Job Wilson Kemp,
to whom God is keeping all His promises.
Bless the Lord, O my soul!*

Contents

4

Promises of God from the New Testament

A Note to the Grown-Ups

Hello!

I trust you have a child you love in your life, one you hope will learn to know more about God and His love. You might be a parent who is going to use this resource at family devotion time, a grandparent who will read the stories any chance you get, an aunt or uncle who wants to help disciple the kids you love to spoil, or (like me) a Sunday School teacher who is looking for an additional resource to use with the kiddos you get to teach each week.

For nearly two decades, I have taught the Bible to adults, teenagers, preteens, and preschoolers. Without exception, the preschoolers learn the most but require the most preparation to teach. When they have the material synthesized for them through a lens they can understand, with context that is concrete for them, they can then learn the great Truths that are certain from God and accept what is yet a mystery about this same God.

That is what I've tried to accomplish in this book. I've learned that the thread of the promises of God is sticky for kids and easy for them to understand. It weaves together the stories from creation to the new heavens and earth, all while making the stories personal. This thread, coupled with a way of teaching that either uses words children know or defines important words they may not know, makes the most complex of biblical stories comprehendible to children as young as three, but fully engaging for children as old as nine or ten.

God has given us all that is needed for children to understand the gospel, the grand narrative of the Bible, and the promises that are ultimately fulfilled in God's people as heirs alongside a reigning Jesus in the new earth. I've written these stories to be read aloud, and I hope that you'll quickly catch the tone that is emotive, sometimes funny, always clear, and imaginative when biblically appropriate.

I pray that every child who is read this book will finish it with a heart that is softer toward the God who created him or her. And I pray that you, the reader, will find the same for your own heart. That by reading these simply profound truths to the little ones you love, you'll remember how deeply you are loved by our great God, who establishes and keeps His promises for His people.

He is good.

And He always keeps His promises.

Blessed be the name of the Lord!

Jennifer Lyell

God Before Light

(THE GOD WHO ALWAYS KEEPS HIS PROMISES)

$\mathcal{D}$id you know that God existed before there was any light anywhere? God has always existed. And sometimes grown-ups forget to tell kiddos some of the most important things about God, like how He has always been around— always! Or how He is only one God, but He has three persons that are all completely that one God.

Now, you're little, and you probably can't reach the top cabinets or drive a car, but did you know that the Bible says we're *all* supposed to think about God the way little children think about God? So that means you can definitely know some important things about Him before we get started with the big, gigantic, amazing story of His promises. This story is better than any cake you've ever had or any party you've ever been to!

The first thing you need to know is that God has always been God. There wasn't a time without God. He was around before all the things He created, and He has always been the same. He doesn't change.

The second thing you need to know is that there is only one God in the whole entire world. Most of the time we just call Him God because most of the time we're talking about all of God and all of who He is.

So that's Him, God. Buuuuuuuuuuuutttttttt, there are two more things *about* God that you need to listen closely to hear and understand. Are you ready to keep going?

Okay, so we just learned that there's only one God. We know that now. But the third thing you need to know about God is that He has three different persons to Him. There is God the Father, God the Son (whose name is Jesus), and God the Holy Spirit. The Father, the Son, and the Holy Spirit are all God. They are different from each other, and we'll get to hear stories about each of them, but they are each the one God.

This doesn't make sense if you think about God like we think about people, because one person can only ever be one person. But God isn't like people. He can be and do whatever He chooses. So, the one God can have three different persons that are each by themselves totally God, but the three persons are also all the same one God. That's kind of confusing, isn't it? Well, it's confusing for grown-ups too, because some things about God are a mystery to us. But we get to understand enough to know Him and to know that He keeps His promises, which is what we're going to learn about in this book.

Now keep those ears open because there's one more big grown-up thing you should know about God: He has always known every single thing that was going to happen, and nothing ever happens without His permission. That means when we hear about something that happened in the Bible, where someone disobeyed God or it *seems* like God's plans were messed up, God's plans were never ever messed up. He knows everything about us before we are born, and He knows all the things that haven't even happened yet!

But guess what? Since God told us some of those things in the Bible and this is a *Bible* storybook, you're going to get to know about them too!

—*FROM PSALM 90, 135*

Questions

* How many Gods are there?
* How many persons is the one God?
* What are the names of the persons of God?
* Does God get surprised or confused about things that happen in the world?

The First Promise

Once upon a time, there actually wasn't time. There was only God. He has been God since before there was time. In fact, He made time! He made everything. It happened like this. . . .

God was good, and He knew what would be good. He knew how to create and how to make living things that would enjoy Him and that He could enjoy. So that's what He did.

At first all was dark and full of nothing. So God said, "Let there be light!" And guess what? There was light. That is all it took to make light in the whole universe. God said so, and it happened. Because He said it. Now, we don't really know how He said those words . . . if He shouted or if He whispered . . . if He talked with His inside voice or His outside voice. But we know that God is so powerful and so good that He can make the best of worlds with the softest of words. His power doesn't have to be shouted to work, and His promises don't have to be loud to be true.

Once He had made the light, He called it "day" and the darkness He called "night." It was good to have day, and it was good to have night. But He is a creative God, and He wanted more than day and night for the world He would love. He wanted land and seas and stars and fish and birds and beasts. And He wanted people.

God made all these things by speaking. He put the oceans in just the right spots to give the earth water but not too much water. He told the oceans where to stay, and that is where they stayed, obeying God's words.

After He had made day and night and the sky, God called for the waters to move back and for dry land to show, and they did, making the land and the sea. He then called for the ground to grow vegetables and fruit, and it did. He knew that He was about to make living creatures who would need land to walk on and food to eat.

So now there was ground and a sky. The ground had plants and vegetables, but the skies were empty . . . until God made stars to fill the skies! He also made two special lights—one to rule over the day and one to rule over the night.

God filled the water with fish and animals that swim! Big fish and little fish. They were all created in one second because He said they should exist.

Just as He had filled the water, He filled the air. With His word there were birds of all kinds flying around! Big birds and little birds . . . and it was all good.

Then it was time for God to fill the land with animals. He called for the ground to be filled with living creatures of all kinds and sizes—cows and giraffes and dogs and ants and wallabies and pandas and gorillas and cats and mice and more! God spoke the word, and all these animals were alive, and it was good.

God looked around and knew that all He had created was good—the land and the seas, the heavens and the earth, the stars in the sky, the fish and the birds, and the animals on the ground. But He wasn't done making the world. One very special part of the world was missing.

Do you know what it was? What had God still not created? It's something He made in His image, which means it's a bit like Him. It was people! First, He made a man. But after God made the man, He realized that it wasn't good that there was only a man. Someone was still missing. It was a woman! So God made woman too. And it was so good.

The man's name was Adam, and the woman's name was Eve. God loved them so much. They were His very most absolute favoritest thing He had made! He loved them, and He made them promises right from the beginning. He told them that He had put them in charge of all the things on the earth, and they would always have the food they needed. He promised He would take care of them. He gave them hearts that knew Him. And it was good!

—*FROM GENESIS 1–2*

Questions

* **What are your favorite things God made?**

* **How did God make things?**

* **What was God's favorite thing He made?**

* **What did God promise Adam and Eve?**

The Broken Promise

God gave Adam and Eve a beautiful, adventurous world. They lived in a garden filled with animals and streams and rocks and fields and hills and flowers. It was always sunny, and it was never ever rainy. In fact, it was so perfect that Adam and Eve didn't even need shoes when they ran through the hills or the fields or the water! It was never too hot or too cold, and there were no sharp things to hurt their feet. These brand-new people had everything they needed, and everything was good because that's how God made it.

God knew what was best for Adam and Eve because He had made them and had made their hearts. And He knew that there was one rule Adam and Eve needed. Remember how God had promised them that He would always give them the food they needed? Well, He told them something else. . . . They could eat any fruit they found in the garden except for the fruit from one tree. The tree was called the tree of the knowledge of good and evil, which is an important name for an important tree. This tree was forbidden. That means it was totally against the rules.

God told Adam and Eve that if they ate the fruit from the forbidden tree, they would die. Nothing had ever died before, but God knew how to make Adam and Eve understand what that meant. They heard God say that not eating from that tree was the one rule they had to obey. They heard Him promise He would always give them all the food they needed, and they understood. So they enjoyed the land and the sea and the animals and the other amazing food that grew in the garden. They were happy, and their hearts were always connected to God.

Until one day everything changed for all of us—forever.

18

19

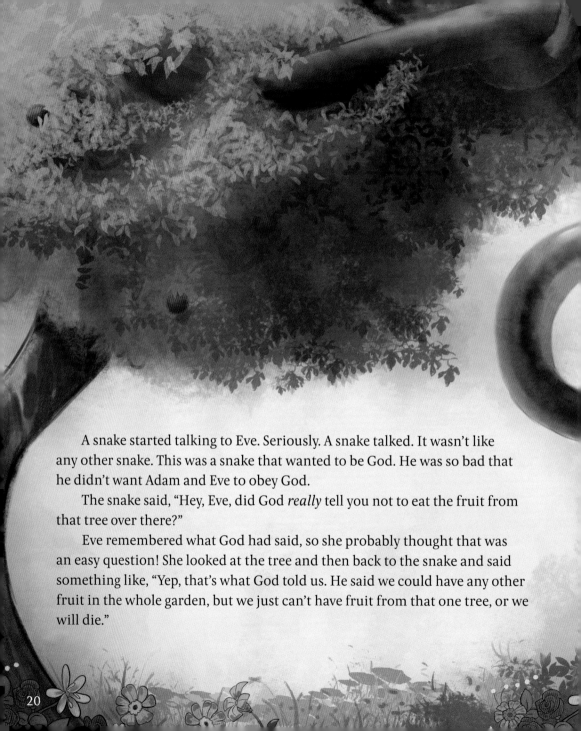

A snake started talking to Eve. Seriously. A snake talked. It wasn't like any other snake. This was a snake that wanted to be God. He was so bad that he didn't want Adam and Eve to obey God.

The snake said, "Hey, Eve, did God *really* tell you not to eat the fruit from that tree over there?"

Eve remembered what God had said, so she probably thought that was an easy question! She looked at the tree and then back to the snake and said something like, "Yep, that's what God told us. He said we could have any other fruit in the whole garden, but we just can't have fruit from that one tree, or we will die."

She had heard what God said and she remembered what God said. Except the snake didn't actually want to know what God said. He wanted to make Eve stop believing what God said.

So the snake said, "Nope, you won't die if you eat the fruit. God knows that if you eat the fruit, then you will become like Him!"

This wasn't true, but you know what? Eve had stopped listening to God and started listening to the snake. She looked back at the tree. It was a really pretty tree, and the fruit looked so yummy. So even though God had told her and Adam not to eat the fruit or they would die, she reached out her hand, picked the fruit off the branch, and took a bite. Adam was with her, so she gave him some of the fruit too. They both ate the fruit. Uh-oh. Of course, God had told them the truth about what would happen. He always tells us the truth. So when Adam and Eve ate the fruit, their hearts were immediately different. They didn't feel that same heart connection to God. They felt ashamed of who they were. They wanted to hide from God. They now had hearts that would die.

—*FROM GENESIS 3*

Questions

* How was the garden special?
* What was the one rule God gave Adam and Eve?
* What did the snake tell Eve?
* Do you think Adam and Eve will be able to hide from God?

A Crushing Promise

God knew what had happened with Adam, Eve, and the snake. God asked Adam if he had eaten the fruit from the forbidden tree. God always knows the answers to the questions He asks us, but He gives us a chance to give an answer that will show how we feel about what we did. But Adam didn't tell the truth or ask for forgiveness or say how sorry he was. No, that's not what he did at all. He blamed Eve, and then Eve blamed the snake.

All this blaming happened because Adam's and Eve's hearts had changed when they disobeyed God. Because their hearts changed, they couldn't truly obey God anymore, and there would be punishments for what they had done.

Oh, they would die. God had told the truth when He said Adam and Eve would die if they ate that fruit. But it was worse than that. Before they died, they would have all sorts of trouble and hurt and sadness. Before they ate the forbidden fruit, there had never been any sadness in the world. When they had eaten the fruit, their hearts had become hard. And hard hearts can't hear, obey, or love God. In fact, the only thing hard hearts can do is disobey God and someday die, which makes lots of sadness. God had made Adam and Eve with soft hearts that were like His and could hear Him, obey Him, and love Him. But now that was different, and it wasn't just going to be different for Adam and Eve. Because they were the very first people and the very first parents in the whole world, the kind of hearts they had were going to be the kind of hearts that all the rest of us would have.

We don't know for sure what it looks like when God gets sad, but He was surely sad about Adam's and Eve's hearts because their hearts were made to be with Him and like Him. But He wasn't only sad; He was also angry. And He had another promise to make. This was a promise to the snake.

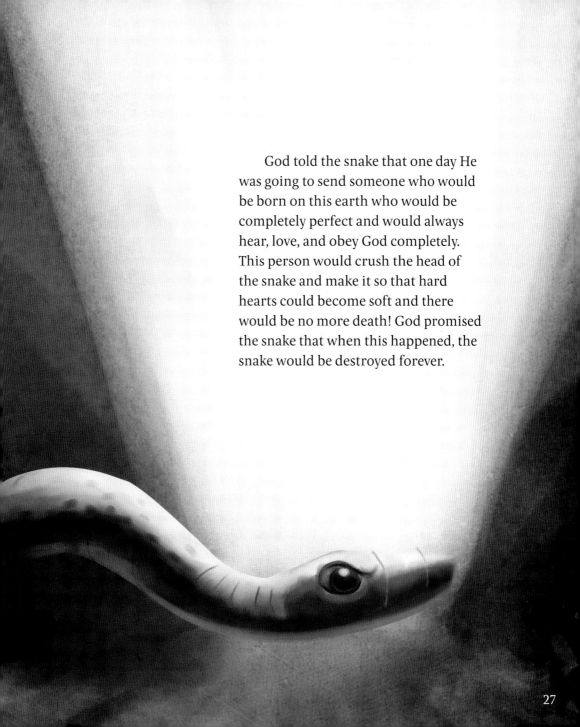

God told the snake that one day He was going to send someone who would be born on this earth who would be completely perfect and would always hear, love, and obey God completely. This person would crush the head of the snake and make it so that hard hearts could become soft and there would be no more death! God promised the snake that when this happened, the snake would be destroyed forever.

Adam and Eve were sent out of the garden, and God was right. They did have a lot of problems and sadness for the rest of their lives. They also had children who had children who had children who had children . . . and all the people of the earth came from Adam and Eve. And all the people had hard hearts because of Adam and Eve disobeying God.

This would be a really sad story except for God's promise to the snake. Here's a big grown-up thing for you to know: God's promise to send someone to crush the head of snake is the very best promise because it means that one day we will have a world like the one Adam and Eve had before they disobeyed.

—*FROM* G*ENESIS* 3

Questions

* **What happened to Adam's and Eve's hearts after they ate the fruit?**

* **What can hard hearts not do?**

* **What did God promise would happen to the snake?**

* **How do you think Adam and Eve felt after they were sent out of the garden?**

Colorful Promises

Lots of time went by after Adam and Eve were sent out of the garden. Lots of people got married, and children were born. But the people did not love God. In fact, they acted like there wasn't a God at all. They were filled with hate and were always fighting and hurting each other. God became so angry that He wished He had never made people.

Except for one man. There was a man named Noah whose heart was soft toward God. The Bible says that Noah walked with God, which means he heard and obeyed God. He had a wife, and he had three sons who had wives too. Well, one day God had an amazing conversation with Noah. God told him about how people were disobeying God and making horrible choices. So God had decided that all the people on the whole earth were going to have to be destroyed.

Seriously. It was that bad. And that is *really* bad.

God told Noah that He was going to make it start raining. It would keep raining and raining and raining and raining and raining for so long that the whole world would be covered with water, and everything would die. But

because Noah had a heart for God and walked with God, he and his family would be saved! God told Noah how to build an absolutely humongous boat that would float on top of the water. And then He told Noah to plan for two of every kind of animal from the ground to come on the boat with him and his family. They would be on the boat for a really long time, so Noah needed to bring enough food for all the people and animals to eat.

Noah followed God's instructions and built the boat. Can you imagine how big it needed to be to fit two of EVERY KIND OF ANIMAL THAT WALKED ON THE EARTH!? And can you imagine how stinky that boat was after a little while? Ugh!

It happened just like God said it would happen. The animals arrived . . . a boy and a girl animal of every kind that walked on the earth or flew in the sky. They all joined Noah and his family on the gigantic boat. Then the Bible tells us that God shut the door of the boat and sealed them in.

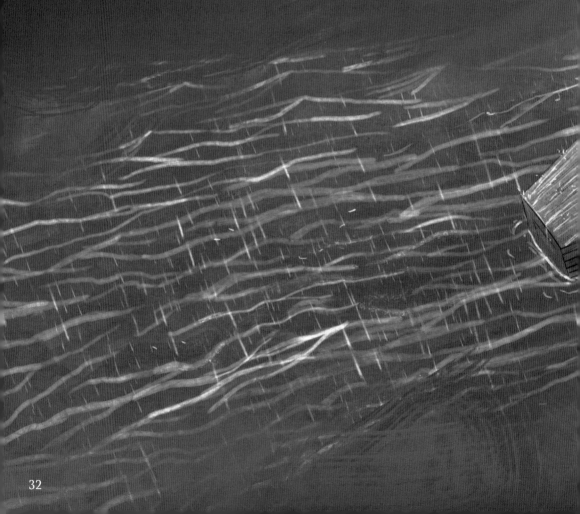

It rained and rained for forty days and forty nights. When it finally stopped, the boat was the only thing left. It was floating on top of the water, which was so high that it even covered the tops of the mountains.

Noah didn't know how long it would take for the water to go down, so for months he looked out the window to see if he could see the mountaintops. Finally, after about ten whole months (which is almost enough time to have a new birthday), Noah could see the tip-tops of the mountains. Not too long after that, Noah sent out a bird three times to see if it would come back or if it would find dry land for a new home. After the third time, the bird didn't come back, so Noah opened the door to the boat, and all the animals and his family went out onto the dry land.

They were the only people and animals left alive on earth. But they were alive! God had kept His promise to save them. That wasn't the only promise God made, though. He also put a huge rainbow in the sky. The rainbow was a sign that no matter what people do, God would never again destroy the whole world with a flood. And that's a promise He still keeps and that we can remember every time we see a rainbow in the sky!

—*FROM GENESIS 6–9*

Questions

✳ How were the people acting toward God and each other before the flood?

✳ What did God tell Noah to do?

✳ What animal would you *not* want to be on a boat with for a really long time?

✳ What did God promise He would never do again?

35

A Promise in the Stars

A long time after Noah died, another man had a soft heart toward God. His name was Abram, and he was married to Sarai. They had always wanted children but hadn't been able to have any. And they were way too old to have babies. So that's part of what makes this story and God's promise to Abram really amazing.

One day God told Abram to leave the home where he had always lived and begin traveling and not to stop until God told him. Abram obeyed God. He and Sarai packed up all their stuff and left, heading in the direction God told them to go. They left home without even knowing where He was taking them. That's how much Abram believed and loved God.

After a very long time of traveling, they came to a beautiful land with all sorts of plants and trees that made food. But this land also had people living there, people who didn't want to share the land with Abram and his family. But God told Abram to take a good look around. God promised that one day He was going to give Abram this land. But He wasn't just going to give it to Abram, He was going to give it to Abram's family, one that would grow to include a son, grandchildren, great-grandchildren, and great-great grandchildren. . . .

Wait. Did God say Abram was going to have *grandchildren* and a whole huge family? Abram didn't have children, and he and Sarai were too old to have babies anymore, remember? Well, Abram knew that, but he believed God because God had just made Him a promise, and Abram knew God always keeps His promises. Abram bowed down and made a special place there to worship God because he believed that one day God would give him that special, beautiful land.

But not yet. God told Abram and Sarai to keep going, so they obeyed and traveled on. One day there was a battle, and one of Abram's family members was taken by God's enemies. Abram knew that God would protect them, so he gathered all his male servants and family members and led them into battle. His army sneaked up on the bad guys at night, and God protected His people. They won the battle easily! In fact, Abram was so successful that the king of the land offered a blessing to him and to God because the king knew that Abram must be blessed by God. After that, God told Abram not to ever be afraid because God would always be his shield.

But Abram was still sad that he and Sarai didn't have any children. He didn't understand how God could make a big family come from them and give them a special land when there were no children to start the family. God told Abram to go outside and look up at the night sky. It was as black as could be except for the stars that glittered all across it— more stars than Abram could count. God promised that one day Abram and Sarai would indeed have a child, and from that child there would be grandchildren and great-grandchildren . . . and on and on until there were more children than all the stars in the sky! God told Abram that those children would be God's children too, His special chosen people.

Even though Abram didn't know how that could be true or possible, he knew that God always tells the truth. So Abram believed God and worshiped Him, knowing that one day he would have a child and his family would live in the beautiful land God had promised to His people. And God was very pleased that Abram believed.

—FROM GENESIS 12–15

Questions

✳ What did God tell Abram and Sarai to do at the beginning of the story?

✳ If God told you to go on a trip and leave your home, what would you take with you?

✳ What did God promise to give Abram and his family one day?

✳ What did God tell Abram about the stars in the sky?

The Unbelievable, Special Promise

God had taken Abram and Sarai on a journey and shown them a beautiful land that would be their family's one day. Abram and Sarai were confused because they were so old, way too old to have babies. But they loved God, and they believed Him. But as year after year went by and they still didn't have a child, they started thinking that maybe they didn't understand what God had said.

Because now Abram was NINETY-NINE years old, and Sarai was NINETY years old, and they STILL didn't have a baby.

Then God spoke to Abram with words that were full of love and assurance. He told Abram that He was making a special promise with Him, a promise that is called a covenant. A covenant is a promise that lasts forever and that is filled with love and can never ever be broken. God told Abram that His covenant with him was that all of God's people from then on were going to come from Abram and Sarai. He told him that kings would come from them, but that most important of all, God's people would come from Abram.

The covenant meant that God would love everyone on earth, but that He would have a special people to be His. This people would someday have soft hearts that could love, hear, and obey God the way Adam and Eve did in the garden before they listened to the snake and disobeyed God.

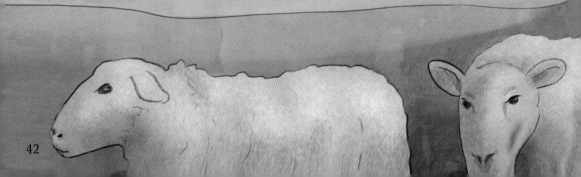

God told Abram that as a sign of this promise, Abram and Sarai would get new names—Abraham and Sarah—and that soon God was going to give them a son, and they should name him Isaac.

Well, this all sounds like pretty amazing news, right? It was . . . except Abraham was super extremely unbelievably old, remember? And God had been talking about giving Abraham a son for a long time. It just seemed a little bit unbelievable, so Abraham fell on the ground and laughed. Seriously. The Bible says that he fell on the ground and laughed.

Abraham told a friend that he needed to find Sarah and give her God's message that she was going to have a son. Well, Sarah was behind the tent door, listening, and heard what Abraham said. And you know what? She did exactly what Abraham did. She laughed too.

God told Abraham that Sarah had heard and had laughed. But God wasn't laughing. God was serious. He reminded Abraham that nothing is impossible with God. And God was right because just as He said, a little while later, Sarah became pregnant and gave birth to a son, who they named Isaac just as God had told them.

It seemed crazy, silly even, for someone as old as Sarah to have a baby. But God had told Abraham that was the plan. One thing we always see is that God does what He says He will do. So just like He said, Isaac was born, and when he was, his mommy and daddy weren't laughing. Instead, they were filled with love and joy because they realized God always keeps His promises, even when they seem impossible. I bet that your mommy and daddy were filled with love and joy that you were born too!

—FROM GENESIS 17, 18, 21

Questions

* What was the special kind of promise called that God made with Abram?

* If God was going to make a covenant with you, what would you want it to be?

* What did Abraham and Sarah do when they heard God was giving Sarah a baby at her old age?

* What did God remind Abraham of after he and Sarah laughed at the news?

A Sacrificial Promise

Abraham and Sarah were so happy to have Isaac. They were old, but God gave them lots of energy so that they could play with Isaac and teach him all the things he needed to know. As the years passed and Isaac grew into a little boy, Abraham continued to love and obey God. Abraham knew that the only possible way that Isaac could have been born was because God always kept His promises. So Abraham continued to bravely obey God.

Before we keep going with Abraham's story, you need to know some words from the Bible we haven't talked about yet, words that Abraham knew well. First, you need to know the word *sin*. A sin is anything that someone does that is disobeying God. Adam and Eve had sinned when they disobeyed God and listened to the snake instead. And because they were the very first parents and everyone came from them, everyone else sinned too. This means there was a lot of sin in the world, and sin makes us separated from God, which is a big problem that leads to the next important word we need to learn that has to do with sin . . . *sacrifice*.

God had made a rule for His people. All sin has to be punished, but because He loved them, He made a way so that they wouldn't get the whole punishment they deserved. Instead of being punished themselves, the people would have to give something special to God that could take the punishment for them. They had to give God one of their very best animals. This gift was a sacrifice. The animals weren't pets. The animals had been kept to make food or become food, so when the people gave a really good animal to God and the punishment was put on it, the people still felt bad. Giving up a good animal didn't feel happy. But sin shouldn't make us feel happy; it should make us give a sacrifice. When the people gave sacrifices, it also showed they believed God would keep His promise to give them food to eat. The people would make a special place of worship, called an *altar*, where they would pray to God and ask Him to forgive their sins. Then they would put the animal on top of the altar and kill it.

This might all sound sort of scary or sad. And it was, but remember how God had said there would be death because Adam and Eve ate the fruit on that one tree in the garden? Well, this was one of the kinds of death God knew had to happen because of their sin. Here's the really good, amazing, unbelievable, makes-it-so-much-better news: we don't have to kill animals anymore because of our sin. Why? Well, God is going to show us part of the answer through this story of Abraham and Isaac.

Abraham knew all about killing an animal to obey God because of his sin. He had learned that God loved him and that God always keeps His promises. And Abraham knew he could trust God. One morning, with all of this in Abraham's mind, God told him to do something that is probably going to sound confusing. God told Abraham to take Isaac, the son he loved so much, up the mountain and to kill him as a sacrifice for sin. Did you hear that? God told Abraham to kill his son. The son he loved so much. Abraham definitely didn't want to do that, but he knew he must obey God.

Abraham told Isaac to go with him up the mountain to give the sacrifice for their sins. Along the way, Isaac was confused and began to ask his daddy where the animal was for the sacrifice. His father told him not to worry, that God would provide the animal.

Up, up the mountain they walked, and God showed Abraham where to stop. Abraham built an altar, where he would lay the animal to be killed. . . . only this time there wasn't an animal. His heart must have been beating so hard, and he probably had tears in his eyes as he worried that maybe God really was going to make him kill his own son.

Abraham stacked the wood on the altar, and he even tied Isaac up and put him on the wood. Isaac must have been so confused and scared, and he probably cried as his daddy raised the knife in the air above him. But just then, with the knife in the air about to come down on Isaac, God spoke loudly to Abraham and said, "Abraham, Abraham!" He told Abraham to put his hand down and to look in a nearby bush. There, caught in the branches, was an animal. Now Abraham could sacrifice that instead of Isaac. God had provided the sacrifice.

I'm sure Abraham gave Isaac a huge hug as he took him off the altar. Abraham had obeyed God and had been willing to give God the thing he loved most—his son, so God said that He would bless Abraham and his whole family and take care of them for all generations. And there was a day coming when God would promise to give them a perfect sacrifice so that we never ever have to make any sacrifices again!

—*FROM GENESIS 22*

Questions

* **What is it called when we disobey God?**
* **How did God punish the people's sins?**
* **Who did God tell Abraham to sacrifice?**
* **What did God tell Abraham when his hand was in the air with the knife?**

Dreamy Promises

*I*saac grew up to be a man and got married. He and his wife had two sons, Jacob and Esau. Then Jacob got married, and he had *twelve* sons. That's right, twelve sons. The eleventh son was named Joseph, and Jacob loved him very much. He even made Joseph a special coat that was fancier than anything his brothers had. Joseph's brothers saw the coat and knew just how much their father loved him, so they were mad and jealous of Joseph.

Then one night, Joseph had a dream that made his brothers even angrier. He dreamed that he and his brothers each had a piece of wheat, but their pieces of wheat were bowing down to his! His brothers thought this was ridiculous. Joseph was almost the youngest brother, so they would never bow down to him! Who did he think he was? Joseph would never be their leader!

Well, guess what . . . that wasn't Joseph's only dream. On another night he dreamed that the sun and the moon and eleven stars, just like his eleven brothers, were bowing down to him! This time he didn't just tell the dream to his brothers, he told it to his father too. Even Jacob was angry with Joseph, and his brothers were absolutely furious.

Then one day, Joseph's brothers were away, taking care of their dad's sheep. His dad told Joseph to go check on his brothers and the sheep, so Joseph put on his special coat and set out to find his brothers.

The brothers were working in the field and saw Joseph coming. One of them had the idea first, but quickly they were all talking about what they could do to teach Joseph a lesson about acting like he was more important. Their hearts were hard with jealousy and anger, and they didn't even care that they were disobeying God. All but one brother wanted to kill Joseph, but one brother, Reuben, said they should instead throw him into a deep, deep hole.

So that's what they did. When Joseph arrived, the brothers took his coat
and threw him in the hole. Then they sat down to have lunch like it was no big
deal. While they were eating, along came some traveling businessmen who
bought and sold things—even people. The brothers knew what they could do.
They could get rid of Joseph *and* get some money! Their hearts were hard and
angry. They were jealous and mean. So they sold their own brother as a slave
just to get some pieces of silver. Then they tore Joseph's coat, put animal blood
on it, and sent it to their father, Jacob.

Their father got the coat and knew this could mean only one thing—Joseph must be dead. Jacob was devastated. He tore his clothes and wept huge tears for the son he believed he would never see again.

But Joseph wasn't dead at all. In fact, he was arriving in Egypt, a land where a king would one day need help from someone exactly like Joseph. You see, God promises that *He* chooses the people who will become leaders, and He had chosen Joseph. The brothers thought they were getting rid of him, but we're going to see how they were part of making Joseph's dreams turn into promises!

—*FROM GENESIS 24–25, 35, 37*

Questions

✳ How many sons did Jacob have?

✳ Why didn't Joseph's brothers like him?

✳ What did Joseph's dad give him that was so special?

✳ How do you think Joseph felt when his brothers threw him into the pit?

The Prisoner's Promise

*I*n the faraway land of Egypt, Joseph was now being held prisoner by the king. But Joseph wasn't alone; God was with him. He was one of God's people, and God had given him a very special gift, the gift of understanding dreams and how they told what God was going to do. Now, this didn't happen for all dreams, but Joseph's special gift was because he had a soft heart, one that was well connected to God's heart. This was long before there was a Bible, but Joseph could still hear God so clearly and know what God was saying!

So not long after Joseph's brothers sold him and he ended up in the Egyptian prison, two of the king's helpers told Joseph their dreams. The men were very confused, but Joseph explained what the dreams meant. He said they were telling what God was going to do in the future, and soon everything Joseph described was exactly what happened. So the men knew that Joseph was a man who could hear from God.

Two really long, not-fun, no-good years later, Joseph was still trapped in prison. But he still loved and believed God, and his heart was soft toward God. Joseph knew God hadn't forgotten him because he remembered the dreams God had given him . . . dreams that one day Joseph would be a leader others would look up to. His brothers might not have liked those dreams, but Joseph knew they were true.

One day the king had two dreams. He knew they were important, but he didn't understand them, so he asked everyone for help. One of his men remembered the time Joseph had understood his earlier dream, so the man told the king about Joseph. The king, who was called Pharaoh, called for Joseph and told him all about the dreams.

In the first dream, seven cows came out of the river. These cows were big and would make lots of meat for the people to eat. But then seven thin, small cows appeared. These small, sick-looking cows didn't have any meat on them, but they *ate* the big, healthy cows! Right after that, Pharaoh had had *another* dream. In this dream, seven really big pieces of wheat came up on a stalk. After them, seven tiny, thin, dying pieces of wheat sprouted up and swallowed the seven plump ones. After this second dream, Pharaoh had become very worried and called for help.

So Joseph heard the king tell about his dreams. Because God had given Joseph the special gift, Joseph knew exactly what these dreams meant. He told Pharaoh the dreams meant that there would be seven years with lots of food to grow and eat, but then there would be seven more years when animals would die and food would not grow from the ground. He told Pharaoh that God gave this dream so that the king would be able to protect his people from starving. Joseph told Pharaoh a plan from God for how to save enough food so that when the seven years of no food growing came, all the people of Egypt would still have enough food.

Pharaoh knew immediately that Joseph was hearing from God. The king was so thankful for Joseph's help that he put him in charge of the plan to save the food. And just like that, Joseph became a powerful leader in the king's house. He wasn't a prisoner anymore. He had been protected by God and made into a leader just like God had told him even though Joseph had been trapped and left all alone!

—FROM GENESIS 37, 40–41

Questions

* **What was Joseph when he was first brought to Egypt?**
* **What was Joseph's special gift from God?**
* **What did Joseph tell Pharaoh his dreams meant?**
* **What did Pharaoh do to Joseph after Joseph told him what his dreams meant?**

The Promise of Providing

Joseph went went from being a prisoner to being one of Pharaoh's top leaders. Pharaoh had beautiful clothes made for Joseph and gave him his very own chariot. In it, Joseph traveled around Egypt, making sure everyone grew and saved enough food before the seven years when the ground would not grow food. Joseph's life had changed so much from the boy whose jealous brothers had thrown him in a pit and pretended he was dead. Joseph now had power, but he remembered it was God who had protected him, God who had given him the gift of understanding dreams, and God who deserved worship and praise. God had given Joseph everything he needed. A grown-up way to say that God gave Joseph what he needed is to say that God *provided* for Joseph.

For seven years, the land made much food, but suddenly it stopped, just as Joseph had said. The land would no longer grow food, and the animals died. Everything was fine in Egypt because God had warned Pharaoh through Joseph, so they were prepared. Joseph had made sure there was food stored away for all the people in Egypt. In fact, he had made sure there was even a little extra stored away for people from other surrounding lands, because he knew that they, too, would be hungry and would hear that there was food in Egypt. Pharaoh wanted to make sure that the Egyptian people got their food first and that all other food was given out fairly, so he put Joseph in charge of making sure that only those who were approved by Joseph received any of the stored food. Pharaoh knew they had to make it last seven whole years or they would starve.

Meanwhile, Joseph's father (Jacob) and eleven brothers still lived far away. They had not known that a time would be coming without food, so they were running out of food and starving. Joseph's father heard that there was food for sale in Egypt, so he gathered his sons and told them to go to Egypt and buy some grain. The father was still so sad thinking Joseph was dead, so he kept one son, Benjamin, safe at home. Jacob had never forgotten Joseph and loved him deeply.

Joseph's brothers arrived in Egypt and were brought in before Joseph to ask to buy grain. Joseph recognized his brothers immediately, but they did not know who he was in his fancy Egyptian clothing. They bowed down low before him, and Joseph remembered his dreams of them bowing before him. He saw that his father was not there and that one of his brothers was also missing, so he wanted to test his brothers. When they asked to buy grain, Joseph told them they were spies! They tried to tell him that they were not spies, that they had money and they had to return with grain to their father and younger brother back home or else they would all starve. Joseph put them in prison for three days while he considered what to do.

While in prison, Reuben reminded his brothers about how they had sold Joseph. He told his brothers that they were starving and in prison because of that sin. Reuben said all this in front of Joseph because he didn't know that Joseph could speak their language or understand them, but he heard, and he understood.

When Joseph heard Reuben speak with sadness over how they had treated him, he had to turn away from them because he had begun to cry. Even though he had trusted God when his brothers had been so mean to him long ago, it still hurt him very much, and those tears came quickly. Joseph still wasn't sure if they were telling the truth about Benjamin or their father. But if they were, well, then he knew what he had to do.

And meanwhile, as promised, God had done exactly what He had said He would do. He had brought seven good years and now the seven hard years, and He had brought Joseph's brothers to bow before him. And now those brothers had to wait....

—*FROM GENESIS 41–43*

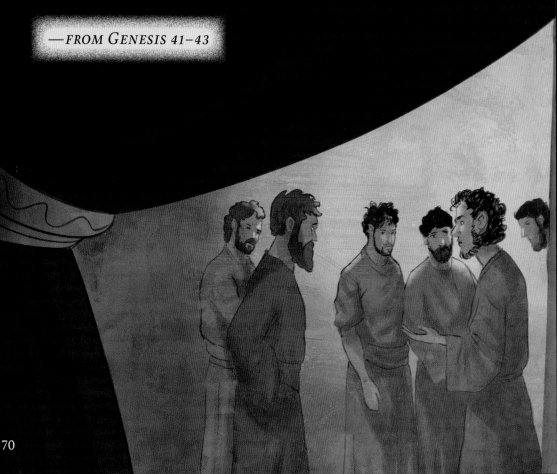

Questions

* What were some of the ways Pharaoh took care of Joseph?

* What did Joseph's father ask his brothers to do?

* What did Joseph's brothers do when they met him the first time in Egypt?

* What do you think Joseph is going to do with his brothers?

A Sovereign Promise

*I*t was time. Joseph faced his ten brothers and told them he would let them go back home. He would send them with grain that they could buy, but they had to bring their brother, Benjamin, back with them. To make sure they came back, Joseph was going to hold one brother, Simeon, in prison. The brothers didn't know it, but Joseph had all their money placed in their bags with the grain.

The brothers set out toward their homeland. At their first stop, one of them opened his bag and saw his money inside with the grain. They were so confused and wondered out loud what God was doing. When they got home and opened the other sacks, they found money in each of them! The brothers weren't sure if they were being tricked in some way and punished for what they had done to Joseph—not just selling him into slavery but also letting their father think he was dead. Their hearts were still so hard, but they feared God. They knew He was in control, and they knew they deserved punishment.

The brothers told their father all that had happened. They explained that Pharaoh's man had imprisoned Simeon and demanded they bring Benjamin back to Egypt. Joseph's father was not about to let them have Benjamin. He had already lost Joseph and now Simeon. He feared he would just lose Benjamin too.

But when the grain ran out, Joseph's father gave up and told the brothers they could take Benjamin. But the father said they should also take a gift of honey and nuts back to Pharaoh's leader, along with double the money. They could tell the leader how the last money had ended up in their sacks. The father pleaded with them to get Simeon back and return with Benjamin too.

The brothers did as their father asked and soon were standing in front of Joseph once again. He saw Benjamin and knew they had been telling the truth. He had a meal prepared for them to eat together, and he began to ask about their father. When they said he was alive, Joseph was overwhelmed with happiness. He looked at Benjamin . . . Joseph was back together with all his brothers. Yet, he still wasn't sure if they could be trusted, so he decided they needed one more test.

Joseph told his men to place a silver cup in Benjamin's bag. Then, the next day he gathered the brothers and sent them back home, along with Simeon. But soon Joseph asked his servant to go after the brothers and stop them. The servant said,

"Someone has stolen my master's silver, and whoever it is will have to become a servant in the house of Pharaoh forever!" The brothers promised they had not stolen anything, but when the cup was found in Benjamin's bag, they all were brought back before Joseph.

Judah immediately began to plead with Joseph not to take Benjamin. He told Joseph how his father had already lost one son and that his father would die if he lost Benjamin. He told Joseph that if someone must be taken as a servant, to please take Judah and let Benjamin go home to their father.

Joseph could not hide his feelings anymore. He told all his servants to leave so that only he and his brothers remained. Once they were alone, he immediately began to weep and cried out, "I am Joseph! Is my father, Jacob, truly still alive?" His brothers were at first afraid because they knew what they had done to Joseph, but Joseph told them not to be afraid or upset. He believed God had sent him to Egypt to save all their lives by being able to store the grain for the land. He said that it wasn't really his brothers who had sent him to Egypt, but God who sent him there. He explained that God was in control of it all and that He had a great plan.

Joseph sent the brothers back home with all sorts of food and told them to bring their father back. Joseph explained that he was now a man of great power and would be able to give them land in Egypt and take care of them like never before. His brothers did as he commanded, and when their father saw all that Joseph had sent—wagons of food and supplies—and when he realized that his long-lost son was alive, the father's heart softened and he worshiped God with thankfulness like he had not in years!

No one ever could have imagined how Joseph's life was going to turn out when his brothers sold him. But God always knew, and God was always in charge. This is a grown-up, SUPER important thing for you to know about God—He is *sovereign*, which means He is in charge of every single thing that happens. He isn't just in charge of what happened to Joseph, He's in charge of what happens in your life too. He already knows every single adventure He has planned for your whole life!

—*FROM GENESIS 42–45*

Questions

* Why did Judah volunteer to take Benjamin's place as a servant?

* How do you think Joseph's brothers felt when they heard Joseph say he was not angry with them?

* What do you think Joseph meant when he said that God was the one who sent him to Egypt?

* Who stayed with Joseph all the way through this story and was the one to whom Joseph always listened?

GOD WILL PROTECT HIS PEOPLE, NO MATTER WHO IS AGAINST THEM.

The Promise in the Weeds

Joseph lived in Egypt with his family for many more years and became a very old man. Around the time he died, the pharaoh he had served under also died. A long, long time passed, and the new king, the new pharaoh, did not have an open heart toward God like the old one. The new pharaoh saw himself as the only king and thought God's people were a threat because they viewed God as their king. Pharaoh wondered what would happen if they all decided to get together and try to kill him so one of them could be king.

Then he had an idea. A very bad, horrible idea. But he was king, so he could make his horrible ideas the rules.

Pharaoh made God's people slaves. He put them to work, really hard work, and he made the work even harder than it had to be. But the people kept having babies, and Pharaoh worried that one day they would grow to be more powerful than he was. His selfish heart was hard toward God, so he came up with an even more horrible rule.

You see, when God's people had babies, there were special women who helped those babies be born. Well, Pharaoh's horrible rule was that those women had to kill the boy babies as soon as they were born. Seriously. He made a rule that babies had to be killed. Can you think of a more awful, evil rule? Well, guess what? The women who delivered the babies knew that God's people were special and that their God was real, so the women would not follow this rule. They kept right on helping those boy babies, and God was very pleased with them.

But this pharaoh was angry, and he was determined to kill the boy babies so that they couldn't grow up and be strong enough to fight him. He told all the people of Egypt who weren't God's people that if they saw a boy baby from one of God's people, they had to take the baby and throw it in the big river to die!

It was a hard time to be one of God's people, so sometimes they cried out to God, but they trusted God and knew He would protect them. They knew the stories of how He had always helped Abraham, Isaac, Jacob, and Joseph. One of God's people, a woman named Jochebed, knew all these stories too. When she gave birth to a baby boy, she also knew the king's rule that her baby would have to be thrown in the river to drown if he was found. So she hid him for as long as she could.

One day Jochebed was near a shallow part of the river when she saw some Egyptian women not far away. She put her baby in a basket and placed the basket in some weeds on the edge of the water. Then she ran away, praying God would protect her son.

The baby had a big sister named Miriam who stayed to see what would happen. Sure enough, it wasn't long until one of the Egyptian women heard the baby cry and saw him in the basket. Looking at him, she could tell he was one of the babies from God's people. She knew the rule, but she felt love for the baby, so she did not throw him in the water as she was supposed to do.

Instead, the Egyptian woman began right then to treat the baby as her son. She asked Miriam, whom she didn't know was his big sister, to find someone to take care of the baby until he was big enough to come live with her. The Egyptian woman didn't know, though, that the woman who got to take care of him a little longer was his very own mother, Jochebed! When he wasn't a baby anymore, he went to live with the Egyptian woman who had pulled him out of the river.

The woman named him Moses, and Moses had an extraordinary adoptive mother because she was the daughter of the king. That's right . . . the same king, the same pharaoh who made a rule to kill all boy babies from God's people, ended up having a little boy from God's people living in his house, being raised by his daughter, and he didn't even know it! But God did. He had protected Moses, and He had amazing plans for that little boy. It didn't matter that the king had wanted to destroy him. No one can stop God's plans. Even if His people start out in a basket in the weeds, with a king against them, God will always protect them!

—*FROM EXODUS 1–2*

Questions

* **What was the first bad thing that Pharaoh did to God's people?**

* **What was the second horrible rule that Pharaoh made about God's people?**

* **Where did the baby's mom put him? How do you think she felt?**

* **Who found him and became his adoptive mom?**

The Promise of Sin

Moses was one of God's people, but he grew up like an Egyptian. He lived in Pharaoh's house and had all the fancy things Pharaoh had to offer. But Moses knew he wasn't an Egyptian. He knew he was one of God's people. And he could see how Pharaoh and most of the Egyptian people treated God's people.

The people were beaten. They were forced to do really hard work and not paid fairly for their work. They were not given all that they needed to live and to work. They were bullied and sometimes even tortured by Pharaoh, his soldiers, and some of the Egyptian people.

Meanwhile, Moses was living a very easy, fancy life. He could just stay in the palace and everything would be fine, but he knew he belonged with God's people. One day he went out of the palace and was walking around where God's people were. He saw how they were being treated, and his heart began to get hard, even hard toward God, because he didn't understand how God could let this happen. Then he saw an Egyptian hitting one of God's people—one of Moses's people—and he lost his temper. He was filled up with anger. His heart became hard, and he did something that God has commanded that we never do.

Moses killed the Egyptian man who had been beating up the other man. He didn't just defend the man who was being hurt. He didn't just stop the fight. Those things would have been wise and what someone with a soft heart toward God would do. But instead, he let the hardness of his heart take over, and he killed the man and buried him in the sand. Then Moses tried to pretend nothing had happened. He went home just like normal. The next day he saw two of God's people arguing. They had heard about Moses killing the Egyptian man and were scared of him. They asked Moses if he was going to kill them too. Then Moses knew that people had found out what he had done.

He was right. Pharaoh knew and tried to kill Moses. Even though Moses had been like a son to Pharaoh's daughter, the king had realized Moses was one of God's people, and he would not let one of them kill an Egyptian and go unpunished. So Moses ran. He ran and ran and ran until he was out of Egypt.

He came to a land filled with God's people and sat down by a well to get some water to drink. While he was there, seven sisters came to gather water, but some shepherds turned them away. Moses came to their rescue and watered their sheep. When they got home, they told their father about Moses, and the father asked them to bring Moses to their home so the father could thank him.

Moses learned that their father was a priest among God's people. A priest was a man who helped others make sacrifices for their sins. He cared greatly for Moses, and Moses was honored when one of his daughters was given to him as a wife. The Bible doesn't tell us for sure, but it seems that during this time Moses asked God's forgiveness for killing the Egyptian and made the sacrifice he had to make for that sin.

Even though Moses had sinned, God was taking care of him. Moses was able to stay among God's people, but he didn't forget about God's people back in Egypt. And God surely hadn't forgotten them either.

In fact, God had a plan for His people, a plan for Egypt, and a plan for Moses. God would always keep His promises to them, even though He knew that just like Moses, every one of them would sin. And all of us sin too. Children sin. Grown-ups sin. The Bible says all people sin. But God promises He has made the way to forgive us when we admit our sin and ask Him for forgiveness. We'll learn more about how He does that when we learn about Jesus!

—*FROM Exodus 2*

Questions

* How did Moses feel about how God's people were treated in Egypt?
* What did Moses do when he saw an Egyptian beating up one of God's people?
* After Moses discovered that people knew he had sinned, what did he do?
* How do you think Moses felt after he killed the Egyptian and ran away?

Chosen for a Promise

One day Moses was taking care of some sheep for his wife's father when he came to the mountain where they gave sacrifices to God. He noticed the craziest thing . . . there was a bush on fire. Except it wasn't like a normal bush fire because even though it was on fire, it wasn't burning up. Moses was staring in amazement when a voice spoke out of the bush and said, "Moses, Moses!" IMMEDIATELY Moses knew it was the voice of God. God spoke to him again and said, "Take your sandals off, and do not come closer because the ground you are standing on is holy."

Moses did as God told him and hid his face because he was afraid to look at God.

Then God spoke again and told Moses that He had seen how God's people were being treated in Egypt. They had been crying out in prayer for God to help them and to save them from the suffering of being slaves. God told Moses it was time to answer those prayers, to bring His people out of Egypt. God would move them toward the land He had promised Abraham that His people would have one day. This land would be flowing with milk and honey and would be a place where no one would punish them for being God's people.

God told Moses to go back to Egypt and tell God's people what He had said. Moses immediately thought that was a crazy idea. How would he prove that it was really God who sent him? God told him to say it was, "I Am, the God of Abraham, Isaac, and Jacob" who sent Moses. Moses still didn't think the people would believe that he had a message from God.

91

God told Moses to then go to Pharaoh and say God had sent him to tell Pharaoh to let God's people go so that they could worship Him. God knew Pharaoh would not listen. God was going to have to do mighty wonders to show His power, but eventually Pharaoh would let them go.

But Moses, well ... he sort of freaked out. He didn't think this sounded like a plan he fit into very well. He started telling God the reasons why it wasn't going to work. First, he thought God was wrong that the people would just believe this was a message from God. They were going to need some sort of sign. God replied to him, "What is in your hand?" And Moses answered, "My staff." God told him to throw it down on the ground. When he did, the staff became a snake! Moses took off running, but God told him to come back and pick it up by the tail. When he did, it turned back into the staff.

Then God told Moses to put his hand inside his cloak. When Moses pulled out his hand, it looked sick and was white like snow. God told him to put it back in his cloak, and this time when he took it out, it was back to normal. God said if the people didn't believe Moses, he could do these signs and prove God had sent him. He also said Moses could take some water out of the river and turn it into blood for yet another sign. So, although God had already selected Moses to be the leader and would keep His promises of that calling, He calmed Moses's fears by giving him these reassuring signs.

Buuuuuutttt . . . Moses still wasn't convinced. Next he told God he wasn't good at speaking to big groups, so he couldn't be the one to lead all of God's people. God answered that God was the one who made Moses's mouth, and Moses could trust Him. But Moses responded by pleading with God to send someone else. God was angry that Moses was being so stubborn, but He was still kind to Moses. He said that Moses was the one He had chosen to lead His people, and that wasn't going to change, but that Moses could tell God's message to his brother, Aaron, and let Aaron speak it to the crowds.

God was clear that He would be with Moses and provide for Him—AND that God had chosen Moses to lead His people. Moses went from a baby in a basket to a man running away from his sin to one chosen by God to deliver His people to the land they had been promised. Moses was a sinner, and he couldn't do everything perfectly, so he thought that meant someone else would be better to serve God. But God still had chosen Moses and was going to use him in amazing ways.

—FROM EXODUS 3–4

Questions

* **What was happening with the bush that first got Moses's attention?**

* **What did God tell Moses to do with his sandals, and why?**

* **How do you think Moses felt when God was telling him His plan?**

* **What were the signs God gave Moses to show the people God had sent him?**

Good Promises and Evil Signs

Moses obeyed God and returned to Egypt, along with Aaron. They immediately went to Pharaoh, and Moses announced that God had a message: Pharaoh was to let God's people go into the wilderness to hold a feast of worship to God. But the request angered Pharaoh, and he would not obey God. Instead, Pharaoh decided to make things even harder for God's people, the slaves. They had the job of making bricks with mud and straw, but Pharaoh ordered his men to stop giving them straw.

Pharaoh thought if he was really mean to God's people, he could prove their God was not God and that Pharaoh did not have to listen to Him. That definitely wasn't going to prove to be true, but God's people were, well, a little bit whiny. They were tired, and they had heard Moses had been sent with this great message of deliverance from God. But so far all that had happened was that they had more work to do and it was harder to do it. Plus, Pharaoh was extra mad at them, which was never ever good.

The people complained to Moses, and then Moses complained to God. But God didn't change because God never changes. Instead, He told Moses to get ready because he was going to see God's mighty power. God said He had hardened Pharaoh's heart, and the king would not let the people go until many signs and wonders happened. God reminded Moses that He was the God of Abraham, Isaac, and Jacob. He had promised to bring His people out of slavery, and He would do so, no matter what Pharaoh said.

God told Moses to go to Pharaoh and again say God wanted him to let His people go. But God said this time Pharaoh would ask to see a sign. So Moses went back to Pharaoh with the same message, and sure enough, this time Pharaoh asked to see a sign that this message was from God. So, Moses did as God had said and had Aaron throw down his staff. It became a snake! Pharaoh was a *little* impressed until he called for some men called sorcerers who practiced evil. Their evil came from that first snake in the garden who had misled Eve. Pharaoh asked them if they could turn a staff into a snake, and they did.

God isn't the only one with power in this world. We learned that in the garden with the snake who misled Adam and Eve. But God is the one with the ULTIMATE power in this world. And His signs are the only true signs. That's what He is about to teach Pharaoh.

God showed His power by having Aaron's snake swallow the snakes the evil men had made. That was a first clear sign that God is the only true God and will never ever be defeated. But a battle was beginning for sure—a battle between God and Pharaoh. Pharaoh believed he was making all his own choices, but he didn't know God had already chosen the outcome. God had hardened Pharaoh's heart so that God could show His power and everyone would know He is the one true God. But that's not all God showed. God also showed that He would let His people be a part of how He protected them. He doesn't need any help to keep His promises, but He lets His people be a part of it, and that is like a promise on top of a promise for us!

—FROM EXODUS 5–7

Questions

* **What was the message that Moses gave to Pharaoh from God?**
* **What did God want His people to do when they were free?**
* **What sign did Moses do, and how did Pharaoh respond?**
* **What do you think God's people were thinking while all of this was going on?**

Plagues of Promise

Pharaoh's heart was hard toward God. God's people were suffering. He had heard their prayers for help and was going to rescue them. Moses had been sent to warn Pharaoh, but Pharaoh had refused to obey God's command and let God's people leave Egypt so they could worship Him. Now it was time for the consequences.

God told Moses to meet Pharaoh as he was going to the river early in the morning. This river or one of the creeks or ponds that came from it was where everyone got their drinking water and bath water. They didn't have sinks and faucets like we have today, so if there was water to drink or use, it came from the ground. God told Moses to tell Pharaoh that by this sign he would know that Moses brought the word of the Lord. Moses obeyed God by telling Pharaoh everything God had commanded him, and then Aaron did as God commanded and struck the water of the river with his staff. Immediately the whole river turned into blood. Aaron then took his staff and stretched out his hand over all the other waters of Egypt, and they turned to blood.

The people did not have water for drinking or cooking or bathing. All the fish in the water died. And it stunk. Boy did it stink. Plus, a huge river with flowing blood instead of flowing water is absolutely disgusting. This was Egypt's first punishment because Pharaoh was disobeying God. God called this punishment and the ones that were still to come *plagues*. A plague is a really bad situation that overtakes a lot of people. Because Pharaoh was the leader of his people, his heart being hard toward God meant that his disobedience toward God led to lots of other people suffering too.

But it didn't end with the water turning to blood. A week later, Pharaoh's heart was still hard, and the people of Egypt were digging in the dirt, trying to find water to drink, when the second plague struck. Pharaoh had again refused to let God's people go, despite God warning him that He was going to send a plague of frogs. Now, that might sound sort of funny. A bloody river is gross, for sure, but frogs can be fun and cute, right? Well, these frogs weren't funny or cute because they were EVERYWHERE. They came into bedrooms and beds and bowls when people were trying to eat. They climbed up dresses and hopped all over everyone. They were all over the place, all the time.

But Pharaoh still said no, and this cycle went on for weeks. Moses and Aaron would go to Pharaoh and tell him that God said to let His people go so they could worship Him. Pharaoh would say no, and God would send another plague. Sometimes Pharaoh would say he would let the people go, to get relief from the plague, but then the hard-hearted pharaoh would show he was just lying after God brought relief.

After the frogs it was gnats—tiny little biting bugs that filled the air as well as their noses, ears, and mouths. Then after the gnats were flies . . . a larger version of gnats that swarmed and buzzed everywhere. Still Pharaoh's heart stayed hard. For the fifth plague, all the Egyptian's animals died . . . but the animals that God's people owned lived. Another week went by, and the sixth plague was big blisters that covered the skin of all the Egyptians. The blisters were painful and oozing with grossness, but still Pharaoh refused to let God's people go. Then God had Moses go back to Pharaoh and remind him that because he would not let God's people go, God was going to show His power to all people through these plagues.

Again, Pharaoh refused to let God's people go, so a seventh plague came . . . a powerful, dangerous, and majestic plague of thunder and lightning like no one had ever seen. With it came huge chunks of hail that pounded the fields and trees and animals and people with its power. Yet still Pharaoh's heart was hard toward God, and he would not let God's people go. The eighth plague was locusts everywhere, eating the grain and all the trees and filling the Egyptian homes. Yet, still Pharaoh's heart was hard. Then came the ninth plague: darkness. When Moses followed God's command and stretched out his hand toward heaven, there was complete darkness for three days everywhere the Egyptians lived. But the light remained where God's people lived.

Moses went again to Pharaoh to plead with him to let God's people go. But Pharaoh sent him away again, refusing to give in because of the hardness of his heart. Pharaoh was hurting God's people, and God would keep bringing judgment on him because of it.

God told Moses there was one more plague to come, and then Pharaoh would let God's people go. This plague was going to be the worst of them all, and when you hear about it, it may remind you of Isaac and Abraham as well as stories you've heard about Jesus. But the story of that last plague is for next time, so for now, be thankful that God has not sent a bed full of frogs or gnats to your house!

—FROM *EXODUS 7–10*

Questions

* **What did God tell Moses to tell Pharaoh to do?**
* **Why wouldn't Pharaoh do what God wanted him to do?**
* **What were some of the plagues God sent to Egypt?**
* **Which plague do you think was the worst?**

GOD WILL SAVE HIS PEOPLE THROUGH THE BLOOD OF A SPOTLESS LAMB.

The Passover Promise

God had sent nine plagues to Egypt because of Pharaoh's refusal to let God's people go. Pharaoh's heart was hardened toward God, and although his own people were suffering from these plagues, he would not give in. But God knew what would change his heart, and this had always been God's plan.

God told Moses to go to Pharaoh again and tell him that if he did not let God's people go that day, at midnight all the firstborn males in all of Egypt would die. The firstborn male animal from each mother animal. The firstborn son from the Egyptian farmer. The firstborn son from the Egyptian rulers. On and on it would go. In all of Egypt, for all living animals and people, the firstborn son would be killed that very night unless Pharaoh let God's people go. Pharaoh was told this, and he had a firstborn son, but still his heart was hardened toward God. He sent Moses and Aaron away, refusing to let God's people go.

But this plague was different. There was a promise for God's people in it. God told Moses to tell all His people that they needed to sacrifice a spotless, perfect boy lamb that evening and then paint the doorposts of each of their houses with the blood of that lamb. They would then all gather together that night and feast on the meat from the animals they had sacrificed, thanking God for His provision and trusting Him with what He was about to do. Then they were to be dressed for travel, sandals on their feet and staffs in their hands, with the blood of the lamb painted on their doorposts.

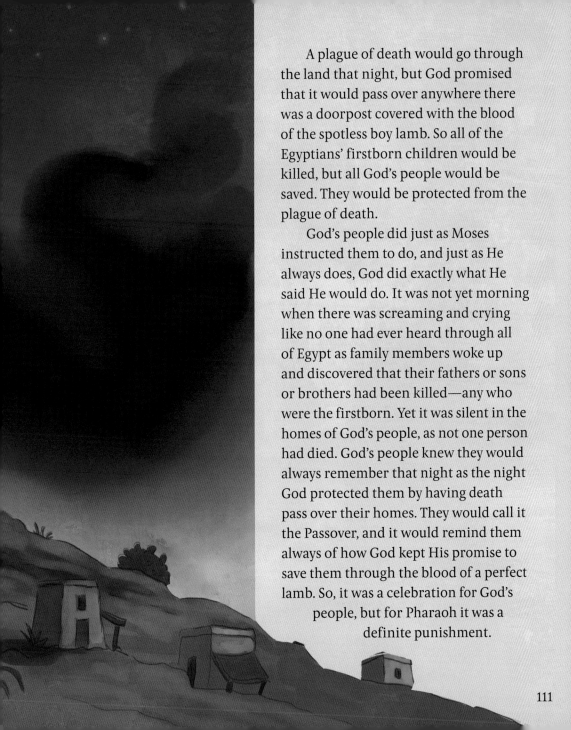

A plague of death would go through the land that night, but God promised that it would pass over anywhere there was a doorpost covered with the blood of the spotless boy lamb. So all of the Egyptians' firstborn children would be killed, but all God's people would be saved. They would be protected from the plague of death.

God's people did just as Moses instructed them to do, and just as He always does, God did exactly what He said He would do. It was not yet morning when there was screaming and crying like no one had ever heard through all of Egypt as family members woke up and discovered that their fathers or sons or brothers had been killed—any who were the firstborn. Yet it was silent in the homes of God's people, as not one person had died. God's people knew they would always remember that night as the night God protected them by having death pass over their homes. They would call it the Passover, and it would remind them always of how God kept His promise to save them through the blood of a perfect lamb. So, it was a celebration for God's people, but for Pharaoh it was a definite punishment.

Pharaoh called for Moses and Aaron at once. He told them to take God's people, all their belongings, and all their animals and go. He told them to be gone and to ask God to bless him. The Egyptians were eager for God's people to leave too. When God had told His people to ask the Egyptians for gold and silver, they gave God's people all they had. And so that very day, even without time to cook food for the journey, God's people all gathered together, and Moses and Aaron led them out of Egypt.

God had spoken from a burning bush and told Moses that He would get His people out of Egypt. God had said that His greatness would be shown even though Pharaoh's heart was hard. God had told Moses that he would be able to lead the people and that they would listen. It had been difficult and scary at times, and it had definitely been gross at times, but God had always done exactly what He had promised. He had saved His people through the blood of a lamb, and now it was time for them to begin the journey to the land He had promised them.

—*FROM EXODUS 11–12*

Questions

* What was the last plague God sent to Egypt?

* What did God tell His people to do so that this plague wouldn't happen at their houses?

* How do you think God's people felt as they were packing their things to leave Egypt?

Pillars of Promise

God's people packed all their things just as He had told them. They gathered together, lots and lots and lots of them, more than you can even probably imagine all being together in one place, to leave Egypt. God led them by being in a pillar of cloud during the day and a pillar of fire at night. Pillars are sort of like tall tree trunks that you can see from a long way away. God sent the pillars for the people to follow because He knew they needed to move quickly and keep going, day and night, to get as far away from Pharaoh as they could, as fast as they could.

This meant God's people had to go through the wilderness that led to the Red Sea. The wilderness was empty land that didn't have anything, but the Red Sea was magnificent. It was huge and wide. God told Moses that the people should camp a little ways before the sea because God was not done showing His power over Pharaoh. He was going to harden Pharaoh's heart one more time so that Pharaoh would change his mind and come chasing after God's people! This would let God deal with Pharaoh one last time and show everyone that God will always defeat the enemies of His people.

Moses did as God told him to do, and God did as God said He would do. Pharaoh gathered all his men and all his chariots and went after God's people. They looked up from the wilderness and could see the army of Egyptian soldiers coming. The people began to cry out in anger and fear to Moses. Why had he led them out only to be captured and killed? But Moses trusted God and told the people not to be afraid, to stand firm, and that they were going to get to see God save them. He said, "The LORD will fight for you, and you have only to be silent."

So the people were up against the huge Red Sea, and Pharaoh and his men were coming toward them. The people had nowhere to go! They felt trapped and scared. But God had a plan. He told Moses to stretch out his hand over the sea. The waters split apart and rolled back to create a path down the middle. So the people of God walked in between the waters, on dry land, while God held the waters back on both sides of them.

The Egyptians charged after God's people, right into the dry land between the walls of water. But God was in front of them as the pillars of fire and cloud, which confused their horses. He made the wheels of their chariots get stuck so that they couldn't follow God's people. Then God told Moses to stretch out his hand over the waters again so that the water would crash back together and cover the Egyptians.

Moses did as God commanded, and God did as He had promised. All of God's people had been able to walk across the dry ground between the sea walls, but the Egyptians were trapped and drowned. This story was told for generations and generations . . . and is being told even now to you, so that all people will know that God is the one true God and that He made a people and then defeated their enemies because no one is more powerful than God!

—*FROM EXODUS 13–15*

Questions

* **What happened to Pharaoh's heart after God's people left?**

* **What happened when Moses obeyed God and stretched out his hand over the sea the first time?**

* **What happened to the Egyptians when they tried to catch God's people?**

* **When God says He will do something, what does He do?**

119

Promises to Pouters

God's people had been delivered from Pharaoh and the Egyptians. They were free! There was only one problem . . . it was a LOOOOOOONG way to the land God had promised to give them, and it was going to take a long time to get there. They were going to have to walk a long time. Camp a long time. And find food and water in the desert wilderness, where there wasn't water or food. That's a pretty big problem for a whole lot of people.

But getting across a whole entire sea was also a pretty big problem, and God had taken care of that. So God's people really should have known that He would take care of them. And at first, they did. They sang a song with Moses about how God had been so faithful to them! They praised God and thanked Him for getting them out of Egypt.

But then they started getting pouty pants. You know what pouty pants is, right? It's when you are upset about anything and everything because you're in a really bad mood. It usually starts because one thing happens that makes you want to sin or not trust God, and then everything just starts seeming bad. Well, that's what happened for God's people. After three days in the wilderness, they hadn't been able to find good water to drink. It was hot. They were tired. AND THEY WERE THIRSTY!!!!! They began to whine and complain to Moses, so then Moses cried out to God.

God was faithful just like He always is.

He showed Moses a log and told him to throw it into some gross, bitter, undrinkable water. Then God would make the water clean and taste good so the people could drink it. Moses did as God told him to do, and God did what He said He would do, and the water was good and enough for everyone. Then and there, God made a rule: if the people listened to what God told them to do through Moses, and if they always did what He told them to do, then God would protect them and be their healer.

As the people journeyed on through the wilderness toward the land God had promised them, they soon found themselves in a place with no food. So guess what? They got their pouty pants back on again. They began complaining to Moses and saying they should have just stayed in Egypt!

Then God explained to Moses that He had a plan. Here's what it was: He was going to rain special bread down from heaven in the mornings. That's right. Bread rain. Amazing, huh? This was a special kind of bread, called *manna*, and God gave the people special instructions about it. They were supposed to gather the manna each morning. They weren't supposed to save any because God wanted them to trust He would give them more the next day. EXCEPT on the sixth day of the week, like our Saturday, He would send twice as much manna down, and then the people *should* save some of it for the seventh day, which is like our Sunday. God was reminding them to take one day to rest and worship, so He did not want them gathering food on that day.

Moses told the people this plan, but they did not trust God, so they gathered more than they should. But the extra manna became full of worms and stank! The people learned their lesson, and from then on they followed God's instructions with the manna. For forty years, He showed the people that He would provide for them in amazing ways, even when they were pouty.

—*FROM EXODUS 15–16*

Questions

* What did God have Moses throw into the dirty water to make it water the people could drink?

* What did God provide as food for the people for forty years?

* What happened to the food if they tried to save more than they were supposed to gather?

* What food would you want to eat if you had to eat it every single day for forty years?

The Promised Land

God's people traveled and traveled for years and years until they finally reached the edge of the land God had promised them. He had shown them many things along the way. He had given Moses ten important rules for them to follow. He had provided food and water, and He had helped Moses lead them just like God had promised Moses.

But Moses was very old, and it was time for him to die. He had been faithful to God, and now he would go be with God. God's people were sad because they loved Moses and he had been a wonderful leader, but they also knew God had chosen a new leader, Joshua, who now would be the one to bring them into the land they had been promised.

The people had FINALLY reached the land God had promised them and didn't have to keep walking. They could eat of the amazing fruit and honey that were everywhere, and they also could gather water from the huge river. It was everything they'd hoped and imagined . . . except for one little—um, actually really big—thing. They couldn't build houses or a town in the land because right in the middle of it some other people who were not God's people had already built a huge city. The city was called Jericho, and it had a gigantic wall all the way around it.

Joshua chose two men from God's people to sneak into the city to find out what the people were like and decide on a battle plan. While the spies were looking around, a woman named Rahab invited them into her home. She was not one of God's people and had been making foolish choices that did not please God, but when she saw the men Joshua had sent to inspect the land, she brought them in and hid them on her roof. The king of Jericho's soldiers heard some of God's men were at Rahab's house and asked her to turn them over to the king. Rahab said they had already gone away. The king's men believed her, and the men were safe.

Rahab went to Joshua's spies and told them that she had heard about how God had delivered their people from the Egyptians and the many miracles God had done. She said she knew their God was the real God and that He would destroy Jericho and give this land to them. God had made it so that Rahab would hear all these things, and then He changed her heart to want to follow Him. So Rahab pleaded with the men to protect her and her family when the city was destroyed. She said she would help them get out safely, but to please save her and her family. The men agreed and made a plan to know which house was hers when the battle began.

The men reported back to Joshua about how it was clear that God was going to destroy the city and give it to them. They told Joshua about Rahab and how they were going to save her and her family. Meanwhile, the king of Jericho had the gates shut so no one could go out or come into Jericho. He thought this would keep the city safe, but he did not know the power of God!

God told Joshua to have his army march around the city once a day for six days. Then on the seventh day, they were to march around the city seven times and seven priests should blow trumpets. When the army heard a last long blast from the trumpet, all of them were to shout as loud as they could.

Joshua told the people what God had said, and they followed the instructions. When the army shouted that big shout on the seventh time on the seventh day, the huge walls of Jericho fell down without anyone even touching them! They captured the city and destroyed the people who were not God's people, all except for Rahab and her family. The spies kept their promise to keep Rahab's family safe, just as God had kept His promise to give them that fruitful land.

God had promised the land to Abraham a long, long time before His people got there. Pharaoh had tried to stop them. Being in a desert without food had made them think they wouldn't get there. And then that gigantic wall had made them think they could never live there. But that's not how God's promises work! No king, no army, no hungry bellies, and no wall can keep God from keeping His promises.

—*FROM DEUTERONOMY 34; JOSHUA 1–6*

Questions

* **Why did God choose a new leader for His people? Who was it?**
* **Who did the spies meet when they went into Jericho to learn about the city?**
* **What did God tell the people to do around the city walls?**
* **What happened after God's people obeyed?**

GOD WILL SEND HIS SON TO LIVE AMONG US AND YET NOT SIN.

Immanuel Promised

Even though God's people now lived in the Promised Land, it wasn't long before they struggled to obey God. When they were in the wilderness, they had known they needed God to provide for them every day, so they had trusted Him. But now that they were in the wonderful Promised Land and had so much food, they took God for granted.

The people had always had prophets, who were men called by God to give His people messages from Him. The prophets would tell them what to do and how to live. They would also tell the people how to fight in battle, and sometimes they would give warnings of bad things to come or share a promise God was making. The people asked God to give them kings so they could be like other nations, which God knew was a bad idea. But God gave in to what they wanted, so the prophets would tell the kings the messages from God.

The people built a city, and they had children who grew up and had children, who had children who grew up and had children, and on and on. They built a temple where the priests accepted sacrifices for sin, and the prophets continued to give them messages from God.

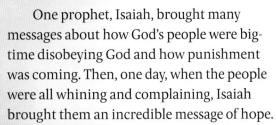

One prophet, Isaiah, brought many messages about how God's people were big-time disobeying God and how punishment was coming. Then, one day, when the people were all whining and complaining, Isaiah brought them an incredible message of hope.

He shared how a time was coming when God was going to make a baby inside a woman's belly, and that baby would be a little boy. That little boy would grow up to be a man who would always say no to doing bad things and would always say yes to doing good things. In other words, this boy would grow to be a man who never ever sinned! Well, this was amazing news because the people knew that everyone sins and that because everyone sins, death was everywhere. Animals died. People died. Even babies died.

And it wasn't just that everyone died. It was that our hearts were made to be fully connected to God's heart. That's the only way we can be truly happy. But sin makes our hearts hard so that they can't be connected to His. God's people knew that nothing would ever be right until God sent someone to fix this heart problem. Now Isaiah was telling them how it was going to happen! God was sending the man He had told the snake about in the garden, the one who would crush the snake's head.

Isaiah told the people that this man would be God's own Son, and He would be called Immanuel, which means "God is with us." He would be God! He would be born on this earth and live like us and eat like us and walk like us and talk like us . . . only He would be very different from us in one important way. He would never ever sin because God can never sin. This was the best message of hope that God's people had ever heard, and from that day forward they began to wait and hope for the time when God would keep His promise to send His Son who would never ever sin!

—*FROM ISAIAH 7*

Questions

* How did the people behave after they got into the Promised Land?
* What does a prophet do?
* What was the incredible message of hope Isaiah gave the people?
* Why was this message such good news?

137

I Promise to Suffer

*I*f you were God and you could make ANYTHING happen, what would you do? Would you make it so that you could fly like the birds or eat any food you wanted? What if you were God and the people you had made had disobeyed you, hardened their hearts toward you over and over again, and were separated from you by their sin? Maybe you would want to just give up on them, destroy them all, and not ever make any more people. Or maybe you'd want to come and show them how spectacular you are so they would want to do great things for you.

That all sounds possible, right? And some of that is probably what God's people were expecting when Isaiah told them that God would come to earth. But Isaiah wasn't done telling them what was going to happen when God came to live as a man on earth.

Isaiah told them that when God came, He would come to do one thing. And this was a thing He would do in a lot of different ways at a lot of different times. That one thing was to suffer. That's right, to suffer. Suffering means that He would feel pain and hurt and that people would be mean to Him. God wasn't coming to be told how special He was or to make sure everyone knew He had more power than anyone else. In fact, Isaiah told God's people that when God came, they would not accept Him—God had already told Isaiah what was going to happen, and God knew that most of His people were not going to like someone who would suffer. They thought anyone who would suffer was weak, and they only wanted a God who always won in the way they thought counted.

140

Except God had made them a promise, and God knew how to keep it. God had promised that He would send someone who could crush the head of the snake. Someone who could make His people have hearts that would love, hear, and obey Him again. Well, remember how we talked about sacrifice and how a pure, spotless lamb had to be sacrificed to make up for the people's sin? When that happened, the lamb suffered. The lamb suffered pain. And just like that lamb suffered, God would have to suffer in all sorts of ways. He would have to do it to keep His promise and to be able to make His people have soft hearts that were connected to His again,

But Isaiah didn't just tell them that God would suffer. Isaiah also told them that God would be victorious. That God would win. That God would make it so that it was like all sin was gone forever! This was amazing news, but the people didn't understand Isaiah. Because their hearts were still hard and because God hadn't come yet, they didn't listen to Isaiah, and they continued wishing for God to do what *they* thought would be best, which was to send a powerful king who would make their lives safer and easier.

Today we don't have prophets like Isaiah who tell us news from God. Instead we have the Bible, which tells us all God wants us to know. But sometimes we don't believe the Bible, just like God's people didn't believe Isaiah. That's why it's so important that you're learning these stories. The whole Bible shows us that God keeps His promises and that those promises are possible because God came to suffer—all so we can be free from the punishment of sin and instead have hearts that love God!

—*FROM ISAIAH 53*

Questions

* **What do you think God should do with His people since they keep sinning?**
* **What do you think God should do when you sin?**
* **What is something God can do that you can't do?**
* **What's a time when you suffered, and how did that make you feel?**

The New Promise

Jeremiah was another prophet before there was the Bible to tell people what God wanted them to do and what God was going to do. He was a prophet to God's people at a time when they were being horribly disobedient to God. They were acting like other things were God and worshiping them, they were doing horrible things to each other, and they kept having very hard hearts that didn't listen to God.

But God still loved them. And He was still going to keep His promise to them. Remember how God had made a covenant with Abraham that He would make a people for Himself and be their God forever? Remember how we learned that a covenant is a very special promise that is filled with love and can never be broken? Well, we've seen how God kept that promise He made to Abraham. From Abraham and Sarah's one baby, Isaac, God made a whole people! Thousands and thousands and thousands of them. And He had a plan for each of them just like He did for Joseph, and He protected them as a group as He did from Pharaoh. He also kept His promise to bring them to the special land He had chosen for them.

Remember God's promise in the garden about how He would make it so that His people's hearts would be made soft again and able to love, worship, and obey Him? Well, the problem was that every time someone sins, it separates their heart from God. It hardens it some. So even when God's people were obeying Him by making sacrifices like He told them to do, the problem was never really fixed because they had to keep making the sacrifices over and over. More and more animals had to be killed because the people couldn't stop sinning. God saw this problem, but He had always had a plan, and Jeremiah was the one who got to give this new message to God's people. It was a message of a new covenant! Now, you might expect a covenant about punishment because the people were being so bad. But it was the opposite!

143

144

Jeremiah told God's people that a time was coming when God was going to make a way for them to have a new covenant with Him. In this covenant, God would make it so their sins could be forgiven once and for all forever and ever and ever and ever! They wouldn't have to keep sacrificing over and over.

Just like when Isaiah told the people about how God would suffer when He came as a human, the people once again didn't understand when Jeremiah told them about this new covenant. They also didn't know that this new covenant would not only be for the people who had been God's people, but it was going to make it so that anyone could be one of God's people!

Jeremiah delivered the promise of the coming covenant, but it wasn't actually time for the covenant to start yet. There was still a very important, very big sacrifice that had to be made before that covenant could begin. But God promised it, and that means it was definitely going to happen!

—FROM JEREMIAH 31

Questions

* **What is a covenant?**

* **What was the first covenant God made with Abraham?**

* **What were some things God's people were doing while Jeremiah was a prophet?**

* **What was the new covenant Jeremiah said was going to come?**

The Promised One

God had been speaking to His people through prophets like Isaiah and Jeremiah, but then He stopped. It was quiet for a very, very long time. Some of His people had written His promises down and shared them from parent to child over and over so that people wouldn't forget them. But they didn't know when it would be time for those promises to happen. They just had to wait and trust that God would do what He said He would do.

Then one day the strangest thing happened. A young lady named Mary had planned to marry a man named Joseph, but she hadn't married him yet. She was still living at home with her mom and dad. She was one of God's people, and she loved God very much. God knew this and had chosen her for an amazing thing that would only happen one time in one place in the whole world. Mary didn't know God had chosen her for something special . . . until one day when an angel appeared!

147

Now, we don't know for sure what Mary was doing when the angel appeared, but she was probably doing some chores around the house. She wasn't expecting an angel that day, and she didn't know God had a special plan for her. So when the angel showed up and said, "Hello! God is with you," Mary was scared. The angel had to tell her not to be afraid because God was very pleased with her. That made Mary a little less nervous, but what he told her next was truly amazing. He told her that God was going to put a baby in her belly—a baby whose daddy was going to be God Himself! God wasn't putting a baby in Mary's belly the way He had with any other baby ever in the whole wide world history of babies. This baby was different because He didn't have a daddy who was a human. Every other baby has a daddy who is a human. This was the only baby ever whose daddy would be God.

Mary was amazed. Then the angel told Mary that when the baby was born, she should name Him *Jesus*, which means, "He will save His people from their sins." The angel said Jesus was going to be great and would be the Son of God. He would rule over God's people forever, and His kingdom would never ever end.

Mary was confused at first because she knew this wasn't how babies normally came to be and she hadn't known that God was paying any attention to her. She was just a young girl, really—was she understanding the angel correctly? But something inside her made her know it was true. It was the softness of her heart that could hear God and knew that the angel was telling the truth. So she replied to the angel that she was God's servant and whatever God wanted is what she wanted!

Later, when Mary did have the baby Jesus in her belly, she went to visit her cousin Elizabeth. Elizabeth was also going to have a baby, and she felt her baby moving inside her belly when Mary said hello. Elizabeth knew this was God's baby and that He was going to do all that the angel said. Mary couldn't help but sing out praise to God for all the ways He had kept His promises to His people. But not even Mary knew that her baby, the one who was tumbling around in her tummy, was going to be the greatest promise of all. God had sent His Son—the One he promised to His people through the prophets Isaiah and Jeremiah—to save His people from their sins.

—*FROM LUKE 1*

Questions

* **What did God think about Mary?**
* **What did the angel tell Mary?**
* **How would you feel if an angel came to visit you?**
* **What did Mary tell the angel once she got done being super confused?**

The Promise of Peace

Jesus was growing inside Mary's belly, and she and Joseph knew it was almost time for Jesus to be born. But that timing wasn't great because a law was made that everyone had to go to their hometown to be counted so the rulers of the country would know how many people there were. That meant Mary and Joseph had to go to the town of Bethlehem, where Joseph had been born. This was a long trip, and it was way before there were cars to drive!

Now, we don't know for sure because the Bible doesn't tell us, but when the time came for them to go, Joseph probably helped Mary onto a donkey or a horse so she could ride and hopefully not be too uncomfortable. Joseph loved Mary very much, and he knew Jesus was God's Son because an angel had come to him, too, and told him all about it. Joseph loved God, and he was honored to help raise God's Son on earth. So Joseph and Mary traveled to Bethlehem. But when they got there, it was FULL of people, so there weren't places to sleep or houses people could share with them. The only place Joseph could find was an animal pen that was sort of like a barn. The owner's animals stayed there, and other animals went there to eat. There was probably some hay and lots of dirt. It definitely wasn't a hotel with a swimming pool or a fancy hospital with elevators!

But right when they got there, it became time for Jesus to be born. Joseph helped Mary the best he could, but it was just the two of them. No doctors, no nurses. Just some animals grazing around and a busy town with a lot of people who had no idea that God's Son had just been born. Mary loved Jesus as soon as she saw Him, and she wanted to take good care of Him. She wrapped Him in some cloths they had, and laid him down where He would be safe.

Meanwhile, there were some shepherds outside Bethlehem who were watching their sheep at night to make sure they didn't get away. Then all of a sudden, an angel appeared before them! Right there in the field! The shepherds were so scared because they could feel the glory of the Lord. The angel told them not to be afraid because this was a message of great news! The angel said that a Savior had just been born in Bethlehem—that He was the One that Isaiah had promised, the One who would bring the new covenant. And suddenly there were even more angels all around the shepherds, singing praises to God! They sang, "Glory to God in the highest heaven, and peace on earth to people He favors!" Jesus was here to bring peace between God and man, just as God had promised!

When the angels left, the shepherds did NOT go back to work. No way. They knew what they needed to do. The Bible says they went with "haste," which means super-duper fast, to find Jesus. They found Jesus, Joseph, and Mary. They told them what the angels had said, and they all were amazed at what God had done. They understood that this was a very important night unlike any other night. What they didn't know was that it was only the beginning, the beginning of Jesus on earth and the beginning of Jesus being worshiped and the beginning of Jesus fulfilling promises God had made long ago.

—FROM LUKE 2

Questions

* How did Joseph find out that Mary would have a baby who was God's Son?

* When they got to Bethlehem, what hospital did they stay in?

* After Jesus was born, whom did angels visit?

* What did the shepherds do when they saw Jesus?

Promises Treasured

Jesus started out as a baby worshiped in a manger, but He didn't stay in that manger for long. Jesus was like every baby in a lot of ways because when God came to live among us as a human, He became all the way a human but still stayed all the way God. Jesus is the only one who has ever done that! So Jesus had to eat and probably got fussy when He was hungry as a baby. He also had to take naps and do chores as He got older. One way He was very different from us is that He never ever sinned. He always obeyed what God wanted Him to do.

Now, do you remember when we first started reading this book and we learned about how there is only one God in the whole world, but how God is three different persons who are all completely God? There is God the Father, God the Son, and God the Holy Spirit. Well, you might have figured out by now that God the Son is Jesus and that God the Father is the One who put Jesus in Mary's belly. We haven't learned about God the Holy Spirit yet, but don't worry. We're going to pretty soon!

This is important because there was one time when what Jesus's mom, Mary, wanted Him to do was different from what God, the Father, wanted Jesus to do. Jesus knew what God the Father wanted Him to do, though, and that's what He did. Here's what happened.

When Jesus was twelve years old, Joseph and Mary and Jesus and a whole bunch of God's people had gone to a city called Jerusalem. That city was very important because it was exactly in the spot where God had promised Abraham His people's land would be, so it was a reminder that God kept that promise. Jerusalem was also where the temple was, which is where sacrifices were made and where God's people learned about Him.

They had all gone there for the Passover, which we talked about when
Pharaoh finally let God's people leave Egypt. When it was over, the whole group
of people began to travel back to the town where Jesus lived with Mary and
Joseph. A twelve-year-old boy today definitely has to travel with grown-ups,
and that was how it was back then when Jesus was twelve too. Only their group
was so big that Mary and Joseph couldn't see if Jesus was with them, and they
thought He was with some of their relatives and friends. Well, a thing about
grown-ups then that is the same as grown-ups now is that they get very scared
when they think they've lost a child. And after a whole day of traveling in the
gigantic group, Mary and Joseph realized they couldn't find Jesus. They were so
scared and upset. They returned to Jerusalem and couldn't find Jesus anywhere.

Then, after three whole days since they had seen Jesus, they found Him in the temple. He was sitting with the teachers, asking them questions about God's law. But Jesus wasn't only asking questions. He was also telling the teachers things about God's law. A group around Him was listening, and they were amazed that this young boy could understand so much about God. (Of course, they didn't know it was because He *was* God!)

But Mary and Joseph were super upset when they saw Jesus. They told Him how worried He had made them and how much trouble He had caused by not going with them as He should have done. But Jesus said they should have known He would be in the temple because that was His Father's house. Jesus was growing up, and as He grew up, He knew the time was coming when He would have to make choices that honored who He was as God and what He had been sent by God the Father to do. Jesus knew He had to obey His Father. Sometimes those choices would not make sense to Mary and Joseph because they were just people and weren't God.

Mary and Joseph didn't understand all that was going to happen, just like many others weren't going to understand. But Jesus went back home with them and loved them well, as He did all people. But Mary knew that Jesus leaving them to go to the temple was important, so she never forgot it, and she held it close in her heart as a sign that God was at work keeping His promises.

—*FROM LUKE 2*

Questions

* **What were some things Jesus probably did as a baby?**
* **What was one thing that Jesus never ever did when He was a baby, a boy, or a man?**
* **What made Mary and Joseph upset and scared?**
* **Where did they find Jesus, and what was He doing?**

163

The Promised Father, Son, and Spirit

Jesus came to destroy death and to make it so we could be forgiven forever and live forever. He knew all this all along, and one other person knew it too. His name was John, and he was a prophet who was born around the same time as Jesus. God had told John it was time for Jesus to begin His work saving people from their sins. To show that Jesus was coming to save people, John was to dunk the people underwater who believed his message, as though they were lying down dead, and then raise them up again from the water as though they were coming back to life. This is called *baptism*, and it was—and still is—a way for someone to show that God can make a way for our sins to be forgiven and that Jesus is that way.

Jesus had grown into a man, and finally the time had come for Him to begin the work He had come to do. He would be obedient in all things. He knew that baptism was one of the obedient things He needed to do. He didn't need to be baptized to show His sins were forgiven because He had never sinned, and He was never going to sin—He is God. But He was about to begin telling people to follow Him and to do as He was doing. If people did what Jesus did, then they would be doing what God does since Jesus is God. So they would be obeying God. Their hearts would be soft and turned toward God, and they would turn away from sin instead of turning toward it like they had been doing.

Jesus knew all these important things, so He went to John, who was near a river where he could baptize people. John immediately knew who Jesus was. He knew that Jesus was God—that He had come to save His people from their sins. John must have been *very* excited to see Jesus.

Well, if John was excited, he also must have gotten really confused by what Jesus said to him. Jesus told John to baptize Him. John said something like, "Um, Jesus, that doesn't make any sense. You need to be baptizing *me*. I'm the sinner. You're *JESUS*." But Jesus replied and told John that this really was what needed to happen. It was a way for Jesus to "fulfill all righteousness." That's a big way to say it was something He needed to do to be perfectly perfect with everything He did.

John followed Jesus's instructions and baptized Him in the river. Jesus was baptized exactly like everyone else had been baptized, but afterward something happened that had never happened with any other baptism before or since. The Bible tells us that the heavens opened and Jesus saw the Holy Spirit coming down in the form of a dove to land on Jesus. And at the same time, a booming voice from heaven said, "This is my beloved Son, with whom I am well-pleased."

Wow! Did you catch that part where it said the Holy Spirit came down? That's the first time we've had a story about the Holy Spirit in this book! Remember how we learned that He is the third person of the one God? But that's not all that's amazing about this because God the Father also spoke right at that same moment. So, when Jesus was baptized, all the persons of God were together right there as one. The Son being obedient, the Father being pleased, and the Spirit being an encouragement. That is exactly how God works, and that's the promise for us too—all the persons of God are always present.

—FROM Matthew 3

Questions

* **Why is someone baptized, and what happens during baptism?**
* **What did Jesus ask John to do for Him?**
* **Why did Jesus say this had to happen?**
* **What happened after Jesus was baptized?**

False Promises

Immediately after Jesus was baptized and felt the encouragement of the Holy Spirit and the pleasure of the Father, the Holy Spirit then led Jesus into the wilderness. When He got there, Satan was there. Satan is the same one who was the snake in the garden with Eve. And the Holy Spirit led Jesus to him! Why would the Holy Spirit do that? Well, because God knew that to defeat sin and death, God was going to have to defeat Satan. So the Holy Spirit led Jesus to where Satan was so Jesus could defeat him. But Satan didn't know Jesus would defeat him. Satan had won with Eve, so he thought maybe he could win with Jesus, and he was ready to look for his chance.

Jesus didn't eat for forty days and forty nights so that He could pray and concentrate on His purpose on earth. At the end of that time, He was HUNGRY. Satan saw a way to get Jesus. He tested Jesus to see if He would do things Jesus knew weren't what His Father wanted. Satan said, "If you are the Son of God, tell these stones to become bread." But Jesus knew that wasn't what God wanted Him to do, so instead He told Satan that obeying God's words was more important than food.

But Satan wasn't done yet. He took Jesus to the top of the city and tried to get Him to throw Himself down so that angels would rescue Him before He fell. But Jesus knew that Satan wasn't trying to get Jesus to show Satan that Jesus was the Son of God. Satan knew who Jesus was. Satan was trying to get Jesus to listen to Satan instead of being obedient to what He had come to do. That trick had worked with Eve, but it wasn't going to work with Jesus because Jesus was God Himself, and Satan is nothing compared to God! Jesus told Satan that God was not to be tested.

But still Satan tried to get Jesus to listen to him instead of being obedient to God. This time he took Jesus to the top of a majestic mountain and showed Him all the kingdoms of the world. Satan told Jesus that if Jesus would bow down and worship him, Satan would give Jesus everything He could see.

Well, let's just say this did not make Jesus happy. No one is to be worshiped besides God, and Jesus came to destroy Satan, not worship Him. So he replied to Satan and told him in a very sharp voice to go away because only God is to be worshiped! So Satan went away.

Jesus had not allowed Satan to trick Him. Each time Satan tried to get Jesus to listen to his voice, Jesus instead told Satan things that were from God. God's words have the power to defeat Satan!

After Satan left, Jesus was not alone. Angels came and took care of Him. They comforted Him and helped Him after He had gone so long without food. This was important because now that Jesus had been baptized and had shown that He could stand up to Satan, it was time for His real work to begin!

—*FROM MATTHEW 4*

Questions

* **Who led Jesus into the wilderness to be tempted by Satan?**
* **What did Satan try to get Jesus to do with the stones?**
* **Who did Satan want Jesus to worship?**
* **What did Jesus tell Satan each time Satan tried to get Jesus to do something?**

A Promise to Follow

After Jesus came out of the wilderness after being tempted by Satan, He began to travel around the area. Many people were talking about John, who had baptized Jesus, because John was telling people that Jesus had come. John told people that Jesus was the one Isaiah and Jeremiah and the other prophets had talked about, the promised one from God who would make a way for their sins to be forgiven forever. Some people didn't believe John, but others believed.

One day Jesus was walking through a town when He turned around and realized there were two men following Him. These men were brothers, and they were following Jesus because John had said He was the One they had been promised. The brothers believed and asked to go with Jesus to where He was staying. They didn't know where following Him would take them, but they knew He was the One they had been waiting for, so they wanted to be with Him. Jesus told them they could follow Him, and those two men, Andrew and Peter, became His first followers.

The brothers weren't Jesus's only followers for very long, though. The next day Jesus got up and went to another town, and Andrew and Peter came along. There Jesus found Philip, who had heard who Jesus was and immediately wanted to follow Him too. But Philip couldn't keep this news a secret from his friend Nathanael. He told Nathanael he had found the One the prophets had said was coming, Jesus! Nathanael didn't believe it at first because he hadn't seen Jesus, and he was expecting someone who sounded fancier than this Jesus was. But he agreed to go with Philip to see Jesus.

As Philip and Nathanael arrived, Jesus recognized Nathanael and spoke to him like someone who knew him. Nathanael was confused because he had never seen Jesus before, so he asked Jesus how He knew him. Jesus replied and told him that even that day, before Philip had gone to see him, Jesus had seen Nathanael under a fig tree. Nathanael knew that if Jesus knew this about him, then He must really be the Son of God. He immediately said so! "Teacher, you are the Son of God! You are the King of Israel!"

We don't know for sure because the Bible doesn't tell us, but it was almost like Jesus laughed a little. He told Nathanael, "You believe because I saw you under a fig tree?" It was like Jesus was saying, "You just wait. You are going to see greater things than this." Jesus went on and told Nathanael that he would even see the heavens opened and the angels of God ascending and descending on Jesus!

Jesus and His followers traveled around the area, and people everywhere wanted to see Him. He began to do miracles, which are amazing things only God can do, like walk on water or make a little bit of food turn into enough food to feed thousands of people. Because Jesus was doing all these things, people began to say that He was the One the prophets had said would come and save people from their sins. More and more people followed Him.

Eventually, Jesus went by Himself to a mountain to pray. He had been really busy with so many people wanting things from Him, and He needed to make sure He was doing what God the Father wanted Him to do. He prayed to the Father and asked for help. The next day, Jesus called all His followers together and selected twelve men to be His apostles—the ones He would teach and keep closest to Him while He was on earth.

These men got to know Jesus, love Him, and learn from Him. And many of them wrote down the things He did so that we have them in the Bible, so that you can know these stories now! And some of the stories tell us about the incredible things they saw Jesus do!

—*FROM JOHN 1; LUKE 6*

Questions

* Who were Jesus's first two followers?

* Where had Jesus seen Nathanael sitting?

* Who did people think Jesus was?

* How many men did Jesus pick to be His apostles?

Promises with Power

When you are sick, you probably want to be in a cozy place with someone who loves you and can take care of you, right? Maybe you want a certain pillow or some medicine, but only if it doesn't taste yucky. Or maybe you've known people who got so sick that no medicine could help them get better. If you're really sick and medicine can't help, then it can be extra scary.

Jesus met many people with that last kind of sickness. Some of them had diseases that covered their skin with contagious blisters that made everyone stay away from them. Others were blind or couldn't walk. One lady had been bleeding for twelve years and couldn't make the blood stop. And a few people had already died, but the people who loved them begged Jesus to somehow heal them.

The crowds around Jesus were huge and pushy. But because He is God, He always knew who was there and what He needed to focus on. So when people came to Jesus, He saw them as God saw them—loved. Many times others treated the sick people as if they were sick because they had done something wrong. Jesus said that wasn't true, and many of His miracles were healing the sick people He met. With one word from Jesus, the man who couldn't walk was able to stand up and walk. With one touch from Jesus, the man who had been blind could see, and those with the contagious blisters were made well by bathing where Jesus told them to bathe.

181

And that woman who couldn't stop bleeding? Jesus didn't even have to touch her for her to be healed. She just reached out in a big crowd and touched the very edge of His robe, and she was healed. Jesus felt the power go out of Him and turned to find the woman. She said she knew who He was and that He could heal her if He wanted to do so. Jesus knew it took a lot for this woman to believe that after so many years of being sick, so He was pleased that she trusted Him, and it made Him happy to heal her.

Then there was the father who rushed to ask Jesus to come see his sick daughter. When they got there, the family was crying because the girl had died. But Jesus knew that wasn't the end of the story. He told the family to stop crying, and then He went to the bed where the girl lay dead. He said to her, "Little girl, get up," and that's what she did! She had been dead, but with words from Jesus, she was alive again.

The little girl wasn't the only one whom Jesus woke from death. A man named Lazarus had been dead for four days before Jesus finally reached him. His sisters were upset with Jesus because they knew He could have healed their brother. Jesus was sad too. He had known Lazarus, and He cried when He heard that His friend was gone. Then Jesus went to the tomb where Lazarus had been buried, where a crowd had gathered. He asked that the tomb be opened.

Jesus lifted up His eyes to heaven and said, "Father, I thank You that You heard me. I know that You always hear me, but because of the crowd standing here I said this, so that they may believe You sent Me." And then He yelled, "Lazarus, come out!"

And guess what? That's exactly what happened. Lazarus walked out alive and well! He was still wrapped in the strips of cloth he had been buried in. Jesus had saved Lazarus, but He had also done what He had been sent to do, which was to teach people what was true—that He was God and had power over death. And it worked, because many people watching began to believe in Jesus.

There's one last big thing to know. . . . although Jesus has power over all sickness, disease, and death, He didn't heal everyone who was sick, and He didn't bring everyone back to life. And He doesn't now either. He didn't come to earth to fix our eyes or our skin or to keep us alive on this earth longer. Those were things He did to show *mercy*, which is a grown-up word that means He was kind to people when He didn't have to be kind. These were also things He did to show He was God. He came to earth to save His people from their sin and make it so one day we can have a new earth with no sickness or death forever.

—FROM MATTHEW 8; MARK 2, 5; JOHN 11

Questions

* What kinds of sicknesses was Jesus able to heal?

* How did the woman who couldn't stop bleeding get healed?

* What did Jesus say to His Father before He told Lazarus to come out?

* Why did Jesus heal people?

185

A Living Promise

*J*esus continued to travel around and teach people and care for people. He was mostly talking to God's people—those who had come from Abraham, Isaac, and Jacob. So, He often traveled through the towns and places where God's people lived. But He didn't always do it that way because He knew the plan was for God's people to grow to include those who hadn't ever been God's people before.

One day He was traveling through a place called Samaria, which was not somewhere that God's people lived. In fact, a lot of God's people thought it was a bad place with bad people. Jesus was by Himself and stopped at a well to get a drink of water. There He met a woman who was also by herself. He asked her to get Him a drink of water, and she was amazed. She knew that most of God's people would never ask a woman from Samaria for water because they thought the people from Samaria were bad.

Jesus began to talk with her about not just having regular water, but having living water that would never end. She didn't understand Him at first and was really confused as to why this man was even talking to her. She didn't know it, but He wasn't really talking about water. He was talking about having life that doesn't end after death.

Jesus talked to her about her life, and she didn't tell Him the whole truth. She told Him only little bits of the truth. But because Jesus is God, He knew everything about her life and told her the whole truth. She was amazed and thought He must be a prophet to know such things. She wondered where the best place would be to worship since she wasn't one of God's people. Jesus began to tell her that a time was coming when she could worship God, but she wouldn't have to worship Him in any special place. Instead, God wanted people to worship Him in their hearts and with honesty.

When Jesus said this, it made something in the woman's heart change, and she knew the things the prophets had said. She said she knew that One was coming who would rescue people from sin and death. Jesus told her that He was that One!

The woman rushed back home and told everyone she saw to come and see a man who had told her all the things she had ever done. Many people believed just because of how that one woman at the well had been so changed and amazed. They had known her for years, so when she was different, they knew something really important had happened.

The townspeople in Samaria found Jesus and His disciples and asked them to stay. He spent time with the Samaritans, taught them, and shared Truth with them for two days. Before He left, they told the woman that they didn't *just* believe because of what she told them, but they also believed because of what they had heard from Him themselves and that He was indeed the living Savior, the One who offered living water to *all* those who trust in Him.

And He is.

—*FROM JOHN 4*

Questions

* **Did God's people like all the other people who lived around them?**

* **What was Jesus able to tell the woman at the well?**

* **How did Jesus tell the woman that God wanted people to worship Him?**

* **What did the rest of the people in the town do after they heard what the woman and Jesus had to say?**

The Unwanted Promise

Everywhere Jesus went, the crowds that followed Him seemed to grow. He kept His twelve apostles close, and they helped Him with the crowds, but sometimes things got out of control. Jesus would go into a new town to teach or just to pass through the town, and crowds would gather and want to hear Him or have Him heal their sick. One day more than five thousand people had followed Him! That's bigger than some whole towns! The crowd was hungry, and the apostles were panicked. The only food they had were two fish and five loaves of bread that a little boy had brought for his lunch. But that wasn't enough to feed thousands of people! The hungry people might get angry! But Jesus wasn't panicked.

He calmly told the apostles to have the people all find a place to sit. Then He prayed over the two fish and five loaves of bread and began to split them into baskets to be passed out to the crowds. Everyone who was there saw that He started with only a little food, yet somehow every single person—more than five thousand—ate and ate so that they were all full. Then at the end, the apostles collected all the leftover food, and twelve baskets of food were left! It was a miracle! The people all began to say that this proved Jesus was the One the prophets had spoken about, the One who would come and save them. Jesus knew that the people were about to come and try to force Him to be king. He knew they may understand that He was God, but He also knew they didn't understand what He had come to do. So He went up the mountain to have some quiet time alone.

That night, His apostles got in a boat to cross the sea. Jesus still hadn't come down from the mountain. The men were far out across the water when all of a sudden they were scared out of their minds by seeing someone *walking* on the water toward them! They panicked and totally freaked out until the man said, "It is Me. Do not be afraid." It was Jesus! He climbed into the boat with His amazed apostles.

The crowd who had stayed behind hoping Jesus would come down from the mountain gave up in the morning. They saw that no other boats had left, and they knew Jesus hadn't been in the boat with His apostles when they left, but they went across the sea anyway. When they got to the other side and saw Jesus with His apostles, they were so confused and asked Him when He got there.

Jesus told the people that they were following His miracles around instead of truly following Him. He didn't say it that day, but their hearts still wanted the wrong things. They wanted what made them feel good or made their lives easier. They didn't want their hearts to be connected to God's heart. So Jesus knew they would be confused by some of the things He was sent to do, things like save those who had *not* been God's people before and give up His own body for them all. But that was Jesus's purpose.

194

He had been sent by His Father to bring eternal life. He promised that *all* those who believed in Him would never be hungry or thirsty again, and they would live forever!

Jesus's words really upset some of the temple leaders. This was not the promise they wanted. They wanted a king who would promise to make God's people powerful. They wanted someone who would protect them and make all their enemies stay away. And they wanted that power *now*. But Jesus kept saying that good things would come in the future instead and that suffering would come first. So it's not surprising that even though Jesus was the One the prophets had said was coming and He was doing all sorts of miracles, some people—even one of His apostles—were thinking about how to get rid of Him once and for all.

—FROM JOHN 6

Questions

* Why were so many people following Jesus?

* How did Jesus feed more than five thousand people when there wasn't enough food?

* How did Jesus get into the boat with His apostles?

* What did some of the temple leaders want Jesus to be?

The Promised Entry

When Jesus was on earth, God's people didn't have lots of churches like we have today. They had one main place to worship Him. It was called the temple, and it was in the town called Jerusalem. God's people were preparing for a celebration there to worship Him, but they were also talking about Jesus and wondering if He was really the One the prophets had said God would send. They were ready for a king!

Jesus knew the people wanted something different than what He was on earth to do. But still He knew He had to begin showing the people what their true king would look like and help them understand how to truly follow God. So Jesus told some of His disciples to go ahead of Him to a certain place where they would find a donkey they could use. They obeyed, and there was the donkey, just as Jesus had said.

They brought the donkey back to Jesus, and He got on it to ride. Now, donkeys are not really fancy animals. Kings didn't ride donkeys. They rode beautiful horses or had fancy chariots. Donkeys were what the poor people rode. But Jesus wanted to ride into the town of Jerusalem, and He wanted to ride a donkey. He needed people to begin to understand that He did not come to seek fancy symbols of power; He came as a different kind of King—One who would make Himself more like all people. And all of this happened just as God had promised through a prophet long, long ago; God had promised that Jesus would one day ride a donkey into Jerusalem!

But the people didn't understand. They were just so excited to see Jesus after hearing all about His miracles. They threw their coats and extra clothes on the road in front of Him as He arrived, making a sort of special carpet for Him like a typical king might expect. They waved palm branches and praised God saying, "Blessed is the king who comes in the name of the Lord. Peace in heaven and glory in the highest heaven!"

The people got it a little bit right, but not all right. By riding into town as He did, Jesus was making it clear that He *was* King. But by riding a donkey and not having a group of fancy servants like a typical king, He was showing that He was not the kind of king they expected. Jesus could have gone to the people and declared Himself king and been given all the power in the land. He could have been given money and fancy clothes and all sorts of people to serve Him. He could have had whatever kind of food and jewels He wanted whenever He wanted. But that was not the kind of king Jesus came to be.

Jesus came to be the kind of king who made Himself low on a donkey when He could have made Himself big on the highest horse. He came to be the kind of king who chose fishermen as His helpers and not those who were fancy and just wanting to get some power too. He came to be the kind of king who would sacrifice for His people, not take from His people.

He also came to be the kind of king who expected people to give God their very best and have hearts that were loving God and wanting to serve God when they worshiped Him. So when Jesus got into Jerusalem and went to the temple, He wasn't happy with what He saw. People had turned the temple—the place where God was to be worshiped—into a place where they sold things and made money, not where all people could worship Him. Jesus became angry and turned the tables over and yelled that God's temple was to be a place of worship, but they had made it like a place where robbers live. This did not make the temple leaders happy at all. They wanted Jesus to be a certain kind of king, and He was definitely not acting like that kind of king, so they kept working on a plan to get rid of Him.

—FROM LUKE 19; MATTHEW 21

Questions

* What kind of king did the people expect and want?
* What kind of king was Jesus going to be?
* What animal did Jesus ride into Jerusalem? Why?
* What made Jesus angry at the temple?

The Promised Plot

Do you remember how years and years before Jesus was born, the prophet Isaiah had talked about how Jesus would suffer when He came? One of the things Isaiah said was that people would turn from Jesus and would despise Him, which is a big way to say they would really not like Him.

Well, God always keeps His promises, and He always knows what is going to happen, so what He told Isaiah is exactly what happened to Jesus. After He entered Jerusalem and went to the temple and turned the tables over so that everyone would be super clear that they weren't supposed to be treating the temple that way, Jesus and His disciples went to the house where they would stay for the upcoming Passover feast.

During those few days, the head priests of the temple came up with a plan to kill Jesus. They had realized He was not going to be the kind of king they wanted, but they knew that a lot of people were following Him. They were afraid that Jesus could end up with more followers than they had, and then they wouldn't be powerful anymore. They were jealous of Jesus, so they decided to get rid of Him once and for all. They despised Him just like Isaiah had said would happen. And, just like Isaiah had said, they made a plan so that Jesus would be beaten and made fun of and then killed.

But the head priests knew they needed help with their plan. And that help was actually easy to find. Remember that snake that talked to Eve in the garden? Well, that snake was called Satan, and He wanted to destroy God and become God. He was the same one who also tried to get Jesus to sin in the wilderness. That hadn't worked, so Satan was very happy to help the priests with their plan to get rid of Jesus. The Bible says that this time Satan didn't show up as a snake, but instead, he went inside one of Jesus's apostles, a man named Judas.

After Satan went inside Judas, Judas met with the head priests and helped them plan how to capture Jesus and how to tell lies that would get Jesus in trouble so that He would be punished with death. The group decided that after the Passover, Judas would tell them where to find Jesus. There the priests would arrest Jesus and turn Him over to the government, who were like the police are today. Only this government made it a crime if you lied and said you were a king or if you didn't obey the government. Jesus wasn't actually guilty of these things. . . . He was a King, just not the kind of king they wanted. And He had told the people to obey the government, so He had not done anything wrong. But Judas and the head priests knew if they said all this, it would be enough for Jesus to be in big enough trouble to be killed. And that's what they wanted.

The priests paid Judas some money to help them, but the real reason he did it was because Satan had told him to, and he was listening to Satan and not to God. Judas just didn't understand that Jesus was God and that He knew exactly what Judas had done.

Judas, the head priests, and Satan didn't know that this was what God had planned all along.

—FROM ISAIAH 53; LUKE 22

Questions

* **Why did Judas betray Jesus?**
* **Why do you think Satan chose Judas to enter and control?**
* **Why did the priests despise Jesus?**
* **What did the priests plan to say Jesus had done so that He would get arrested?**

The Promised Servant

Jesus and His apostles gathered in a large room to eat the Passover meal. But Jesus wasn't there only for the meal. He was their teacher, after all, and He knew there wasn't much time left to teach them.

So while they were still at the table, Jesus got up and filled a large bowl with water. Then He got a towel and—one by one—began washing each apostle's feet with the water. Washing someone's feet was something that servants did for their masters. It wasn't something that teachers and kings did for their students or friends. And it definitely wasn't something the apostles thought the Promised One would do for those He came to save. But this was just like when Jesus chose to ride the donkey. He wasn't going to be the kind of Savior or King people expected.

When Jesus got to Peter's feet, Peter couldn't handle it. He loved Jesus, and He knew that Jesus was God. He couldn't let God wash his dirty, old, nasty feet! Peter said there was no way Jesus could wash Peter's feet, but that instead Peter would wash Jesus's feet. But Jesus had an answer for that and said that if Peter didn't let Jesus wash his feet, then Peter couldn't have anything to do with Jesus ever again. Well, that sure changed Peter's mind! Peter then told Jesus not just to wash his feet, but his head and his hands! Peter loved Jesus so much, but Jesus knew that Peter's love was big but wobbly, so sometimes it would fail. But that was okay because Jesus saw Peter's heart and knew that it was so soft toward God and that Peter really wanted to love, hear, and obey God. This was exactly the kind of heart that could stay connected to God's and that pleased Jesus very much.

After Jesus finished washing the apostles' feet, He explained that what He had just done was an example for them. He told them that all that had been promised by the prophets was about to happen, and one of the apostles had betrayed Him. He explained that as all of the promises were being fulfilled, there was going to be a new way for them to live. No longer would they celebrate the Passover; instead, they would celebrate Jesus's death. They would eat bread to remember His body, and they would drink wine to remember His blood.

But more than that, Jesus told them that they must serve and love one another, as He had done by washing their feet. For so long God's people had wanted power so they could make sure no one would hurt them or enslave them like Pharaoh had so many years before. But Jesus said a new time was coming, a time when His people would be known by how they loved one another and served one another. Just like God's love doesn't ever end—it is everlasting—Jesus wants our love for each other to be everlasting.

The disciples were scared and confused by Jesus's words, and they began to ask Him all sorts of questions. Jesus wanted them to understand enough so that when things began to happen, they would remember; but it wasn't time for them to understand everything yet, so He still didn't tell them everything. He did tell them some very important things. He was going to be leaving them soon, and where He was going, they would not be able to go right away. But one day they would be there with Him, and He would have a place there waiting for them.

And then Jesus told the disciples the greatest thing of all—that whoever had seen Him had seen the Father because they were one. Jesus was God. He was the Promised One, and they were about to see God fulfill all His promises through Him!

—*FROM JOHN 13*

Questions

* **What did Jesus do to the disciples at the Passover meal?**
* **Who didn't want Jesus to do this to him? Why not?**
* **What did Jesus tell them that He was teaching them to do and be by washing their feet?**
* **What did Jesus tell them was about to happen?**

The Promised Deliverer Delivered to Death

After Jesus shared the Passover with His apostles, washed their feet, and told them about the things that would happen soon, He took them to a garden so He could pray. Jesus asked Peter, John, and James to keep watch while He went deeper into the garden.

Jesus knew He would soon be killed. Although He was willing to give His life, He was filled with sadness. He prayed to God the Father and asked if there might be some other way to do what He was about to do. Some other way that people's sins could be forgiven, their hearts made soft toward God again, the snake crushed, and death defeated. But then He told His Father He would do whatever His Father knew was best.

Jesus prayed off and on throughout the night, checking on the disciples, who kept falling asleep instead of also praying. But Jesus knew what was to come. He told them to be careful about things like falling asleep if Jesus had told them to stay awake, because a time was coming when they would have to watch and pray so that they wouldn't listen to the wrong voice and sin.

Then the time came that Jesus knew was coming. The time when Judas would come and turn Him over to be arrested. And sure enough, that is what happened. Judas had told the soldiers how to know which one was Jesus, so when Judas and a mob of people arrived with the soldiers, they quickly went to grab Jesus. Peter took one of their swords and tried to fight back, even cutting an ear off one of the soldiers! But Jesus sharply told Peter to stop and not fight because this was God's will for Jesus to be arrested.

The soldiers took Jesus to the head priests to be questioned. The priests lied and said Jesus had broken some law so that they could punish Him with death. But no matter what questions they asked, they couldn't find anything He had actually done wrong. Then the high priest asked Jesus the big question . . . if He was the One who was promised to come, the One who was the Son of God. Jesus answered that yes, He was, and that they would see Him one day seated on the throne ruling over all at the right hand of God the Father.

Well, that was enough. The high priest was so angry that he began to tear his clothes. This man, this Jesus, could not be the Promised One! The Promised One was going to be a mighty king who would never ride a donkey or hang around fishermen or care for the sick. The Promised One would only want to be with the head priests and to give them all the special things the head priests thought they deserved. The high priest was so angry that he said Jesus's words were a crime that had to be punished by death!

The priests couldn't actually kill Jesus. They needed the government to do that, so they took Jesus to a man named Pilate, who was in charge of the city. He was the one who decided whether someone deserved to die for a crime or not. They told Pilate who Jesus had claimed to be and that as the leaders of God's people, the head priests wanted Jesus to be killed.

Now Pilate wasn't one of God's people, so he was curious about why these head priests were so upset about Jesus. He questioned Jesus and asked Him if He was the Son of God as they said. He asked Him if He was the King of God's people. But Jesus didn't answer Him, so Pilate decided He would leave it up to God's people whether or not to kill Jesus.

Pilate went out to the crowd and asked them if they wanted him to release Jesus or to release another prisoner who had killed someone. Whomever Pilate released would be free, and whomever he did not release would be killed. The crowd shouted to release the murderer and to kill Jesus.

So that is what Pilate did.

And when he did, God was keeping His promise to send a Deliverer to save His people from their sins.

—*FROM MARK 14–15; JOHN 18*

Questions

* **Where did Jesus go after the Passover?**
* **What did Jesus pray while He was there?**
* **When Jesus was arrested, did He fight back?**
* **What did Jesus say that made the high priest tear his clothes in anger?**

The Dark Promise

After the crowd told Pilate to crucify Jesus, the soldiers took Jesus to a room where they began to get Him ready to be killed. They made fun of Him, saying that He was the King of God's people by putting a purple robe on Him like a king might wear. Then they took some branches with sharp, cutting thorns and twisted them into a crown. They pushed the crown down hard on Jesus's head so that the thorns cut His skin deeply and hurt Him. But they didn't stop. They beat Jesus with sticks and spit on Him. Through all of this, He was silent and did not fight back. Then they took the purple robe off Him and put His own clothes back on Him to take Him out to be put to death.

The way Jesus was going to die was called *crucifixion*, and it was the worst possible way someone could die. Two huge pieces of wood were nailed together to make a cross shape. Soldiers would actually nail a prisoner's hands and feet onto the wood, attaching the prisoner to the cross. Then, he would hang there until his body was not able to breathe anymore because our bodies weren't made to be hung on crosses of wood.

That is what happened to Jesus. The soldiers nailed Him to a cross between two other men who were also crucified that day. The painful crown of thorns was still on His head. A crowd gathered while He hung there on the cross because this isn't a death that happens fast. It is slow and painful and horrible to watch and was especially horrible for Jesus because people kept yelling mean things at Him. You might even be feeling really sad right now reading or listening to this. But have hope because remember that this was God's plan, and God's plans actually always turn out to be good. So even though Jesus was crucified and had to die, God was keeping His promises.

After Jesus was on the cross several hours (a very long time to be made fun of and to hurt so badly), the Bible says that it became dark over the whole land. And then a few hours later, Jesus cried out saying, "My God, my God, why have You forsaken me?" Then He let out a loud cry and breathed His last breath. He was dead on the cross. And right when this happened, the temple curtain that separated God's people from the presence of God was torn in half. There was also a great earthquake across the land, and many rocks split, and some of God's people who had been dead immediately came back to life.

The soldiers who saw this all were amazed and scared. They said to each other, "Surely He was the Son of God!"

Jesus's disciples had been there and seen the whole thing, and they were sadder than sad had ever been. They gathered Jesus's body and wrapped it carefully and with much love. Then they placed His body inside a tomb, which is kind of like a cave where people are buried. The soldiers made them put a huge rock in front of the tomb, one that it took many strong men to move.

The soldiers who saw Jesus die were right, of course. He was the Son of God. And now He was dead. How could that be? How could God die? Why would God die?

Well, remember in the garden when God told Adam and Eve that if they ate from the forbidden tree, death would come? Death had now come to the Son of God, but it had come for a reason. And it had come to show that death would be destroyed by the Son of God.

—FROM ISAIAH 53; MARK 15; MATTHEW 27

Questions

❋ **How did the soldiers treat Jesus before He was crucified? What were some of the things they did to Him?**

❋ **While He was on the cross, did Jesus yell at the people or try to get off the cross?**

❋ **What happened after Jesus died?**

❋ **How do you think the disciples felt watching Jesus on the cross? How do you feel thinking about it?**

GOD WILL CRUSH THE HEAD OF THE SNAKE AND DEFEAT DEATH.

The Promised Redeemer

Many, many, many, many, many years before Jesus was born, lived, and died, there lived a man named Job. Job loved God very much. And God loved Job very much. Job had many wonderful things—a wife, ten children, many animals, and lots of servants. Satan, the one who had been that snake in the garden, told God that Job only loved God because Job had such happy things. God knew that wasn't true, so He allowed Satan to take nearly all those things away from Job to show that Job would still love God. And that's what happened. Job suffered, but in the end, Job praised God and said he could do so because, "I know that my Redeemer lives and one day He will stand upon the earth."

Well, Job didn't live on the earth at the same time Jesus lived on the earth, but Job was right. *Redeemer* is a word that describes someone who fixes something that has been broken. Job knew that this world was broken by the sin that Adam and Eve started in the garden. They made it so our hearts are hard toward God and so that we can't love, hear, and obey Him like we are supposed to. Our hard hearts make us sin by not obeying Him. So for years and years, God's people had to make sacrifices of animals to try to redeem themselves. But it never worked forever. It only helped for a little while.

God had promised a way for the problem of our sin and separation from God to be fixed forever and ever. Job knew that way would one day be the Redeemer who would live on earth.

226

Well, that Redeemer was Jesus, but remember how we talked about Him dying on the cross and being buried in a tomb? That definitely happened. Jesus was dead. And He stayed dead for a couple of days. But on the third day, something amazing happened.

His heart started beating.

His eyes opened.

He moved His arms and His legs.

He tore off the strips of cloth they had wrapped Him in.

And Jesus, the Redeemer, the Son of God who had been dead, walked out of the tomb completely alive.

Some time later, two women who had been followers of Jesus went to see the tomb. They were still so sad and thought just being near Jesus's body would make them feel better. As they got to the tomb, there was another earthquake, and an angel appeared who had a face that shone like lightning. He had rolled back the stone, was sitting on top of it, and announced that Jesus was not there because He had risen from the dead. The angel told them to go and see that the tomb was empty and then go tell His disciples that Jesus was alive and would see them soon.

The women did as the angel commanded and were filled with joy as they did. And as they left, they saw Jesus! They immediately fell at His feet and worshiped Him because they knew He was God. He was the Redeemer. He had beaten death just like God had promised would happen all the way back in the garden. The head of the snake was crushed.

Jesus told the women to hurry and tell His disciples the good news that He was alive. The women obeyed, praising their great God who keeps His promises!

—*FROM JOB 19; MATTHEW 28*

Questions

✳ **What happened to Job?**

✳ **Whom did Job say he believed would come and would live?**

✳ **What happened to Jesus after a couple of days dead in the tomb?**

✳ **Who came to see the tomb and found out Jesus was alive?**

231

A Growing Promise

The women who had seen Jesus hurried to tell His disciples that He was alive. Everyone got very excited, although some of the men couldn't believe it. They thought it was too good to be true! Peter went running back to the tomb to see for himself whether Jesus's body was gone. Then he told the others that it was true—Jesus was alive!

That same day, two of Jesus's followers were walking and talking about all that had happened. Suddenly Jesus began walking with them, but He made it so they couldn't recognize Him at first. He asked them what they were talking about, and they told Him about Jesus who had been crucified but was now gone from the tomb. Jesus began explaining to them all of the promises of God from Moses to the prophets, right up to that very minute, but they still didn't realize it was Jesus.

When they got to town, the two men pleaded with Jesus to go with them to where they were going. They wanted to hear more from this teacher. He agreed, and as they got ready to eat, He sat at the table with them, blessed the food, and then made it so they could see that He was Jesus. They were amazed, but just then He disappeared! So the men got up right then and went to find the disciples to tell them that it was true and they had seen Jesus too.

As they were telling the disciples, Jesus appeared among them and said, "Peace to you!" But they were all a little bit freaked out and scared because He just appeared in the middle of the room without walking through a door! Jesus knew what was going on in their hearts, so He asked them why they were afraid, and then He held up his hands and pointed to His feet, where they could see the nail holes. He told them to touch Him and see that He was real and had skin and bones just like them. They were amazed and filled with joy and hope again.

Then Jesus said that He was hungry and asked for something to eat! The disciples gave Him some bread, and then He began to teach them like He never had before. He explained all the plans and promises of God from the beginning until then and began to share with them the plans He had for them.

Jesus told them that He would be leaving to go with His Father, but that He would send a Helper, the Holy Spirit, who was also God. The Holy Spirit would be inside all of Jesus's followers and would help them do what God asked them to do. Jesus explained that now that He was leaving, it would be the work of the disciples to tell other people all over the world about Jesus. God would give them strength to tell about the plans and promises of God. He would use them to grow a whole new group of people who believed that Jesus was the Promised One who took the punishment for our sins and beat death.

Jesus said to go and tell all people, not just those who had already been God's people. He said to teach everyone all about how to be forgiven of their sins and to baptize them just as He had been baptized. And Jesus said He would be with them in Spirit forever.

Soon after, as they watched, He began to rise up in the air until He was higher than the houses and the trees and the clouds. They watched as He went up to heaven to be with His Father. His work on earth was done, and now God would use His disciples to make a new people to love, worship, and obey Him because of what Jesus had been able to do.

—FROM LUKE 24; JOHN 20

Questions

* Did everyone believe that Jesus was really alive?

* What did Jesus ask the disciples to give Him?

* What did Jesus tell them was their job once He was gone?

* Where did Jesus go?

A Helping Promise

Jesus had told the disciples He was sending the Holy Spirit to fill them. The Holy Spirit would help them tell people about Jesus and how to be forgiven of their sins. Not long after Jesus had gone up to heaven, the disciples were meeting together when all of a sudden, there was a really crazy rushing woooooooshhhhhhh sound and a strong wind that filled the inside of the whole house. Nothing like that had ever happened anywhere ever before.

The disciples started talking to figure out what had happened, but when they spoke, they were all speaking different languages—even languages they had never heard or known before! While they were talking in all these languages and after that huge wind and super loud woooooooshhhhhhh sound had come, people came running from the town to see what was happening. They could hear all the noise from far away. Lots of them were from other places that spoke different languages than what the disciples spoke, but each person who came was hearing the disciples speak in his or her own language! The people were astonished, which is a grown-up way to say that they were extremely surprised and confused and excited all rolled together in one.

Some of the people began to ask what it meant and wondered if it had to do with Jesus; others just made fun of the disciples. But the disciples knew what it meant. They knew the time had come for them to do what Jesus had told them to do. They were to begin teaching people what He had taught them.

So Peter went first. While the other disciples stood with him, he raised his voice and spoke to the crowd. He told the people that they could hear and understand the different languages because of a miracle from Jesus, the One they had crucified but who had come back to life and was now in heaven with God the Father. Peter told them that Jesus was the Promised One they had heard about from the start of time and that they were responsible for killing Him. But Peter didn't stop there. He could have just made the people feel bad for killing Jesus. After all, Peter loved Jesus, and they really had killed Him.

But Peter knew that loving Jesus meant he needed to love other people, even people who didn't love Jesus and didn't love Peter. So when they asked

what they should do, Peter didn't say mean things to them. Instead, he told them how they could begin following Jesus even after He was gone. He said they should stop following their made-up gods and start following the one true God who had created the world and who was God the Father, Jesus, and the Holy Spirit. They needed to turn away from their old ways of doing things and instead start following what Jesus taught. This would prove they were trusting Jesus to forgive them of their sins. Peter told them to be baptized in the name of Jesus as a sign of being forgiven; then they would receive the Holy Spirit in them too!

Can you believe it? God's promise wasn't just for Jesus's first disciples. They weren't supposed to be the only ones to tell people about Him and to be filled with the Holy Spirit. God promised the Holy Spirit to everyone who asked Jesus to forgive them of their sins and trusted Him to do so. God would let all those people tell other people about Jesus. That's still what we do today . . . in fact, that's what we're doing in this book that you're reading!

Thousands of people (which is a whole lot) were listening to Peter that day and did what he said. They turned from their old ways and turned toward God, trusting that Jesus would forgive their sins. They were baptized and filled with the Holy Spirit. And then they began telling others, who told others, who told others. Everyone shared all the things Jesus had taught, and His disciples wrote many of those things down, which is what we have in the Bible that teaches us today.

—FROM ACTS 1–2

Questions

* Whom did Jesus say He was sending to be the Helper?
* What happened when the Holy Spirit came?
* What did Peter tell the crowd of people who came that they should do?
* How do you think the disciples felt when they saw all those people deciding to follow Jesus and be baptized?

243

Promising to Save a Killer

God's people, the followers of Jesus, were spreading all over the world. They were telling how God had kept His promise. He had sent the One who crushed the head of the snake and made it so that people could be forgiven of their sins and filled with the Holy Spirit. Many, many people were believing and following Jesus.

This made lots of people really happy. But it made some people very angry. Remember those high priests who wanted Jesus to be crucified? Well, a lot of them and a lot of the people they had taught had very hard hearts toward those who followed Jesus. In fact, their hearts were so hard that some of them were actually killing the people who followed Jesus.

One of those angry men was named Saul. He had been at Jesus's crucifixion, and he had as hard a heart as you can imagine toward Jesus and His followers. Saul traveled all around looking for people who followed Jesus so that he could *persecute* them, which is a grown-up way of saying he would hurt them or even kill them. Saul had hurt so many people that everyone knew to be on the lookout because he might kill you if he found out you followed Jesus.

Now, God has all the power in the whole world, and He can do anything. So He could have just killed Saul. He could have made Saul's heart stop while he was sleeping. He could have had a whole herd of horses run him over. But God had different plans for Saul. His plans were to show how powerful He is by taking the man with the hardest of hearts and changing it to be one of the softest of hearts that loved Jesus so much. This guy who had been going around killing people who followed Jesus was about to become someone who was going to follow Jesus. Except he didn't know it.

245

Saul and his helpers were traveling to another city, looking for some followers of Jesus to kill. All of a sudden a bright light appeared, and a loud voice boomed, "Saul, Saul, why are you persecuting Me?" Saul immediately fell to the ground and said, "Who are You?" The voice said, "I am Jesus, whom you are persecuting." Uh-oh. Now Saul knew the truth. Jesus really was the Son of God, and Saul had been going around hurting His followers. Before he could worry too much, though, Jesus told him to get up and go to the city, where he'd be told what to do.

When Saul stood up to obey, he could no longer see. He was blind! His helpers had to get him to the city, where for three days Saul couldn't see and also didn't eat or drink at all. The Bible doesn't say for sure, but he probably didn't eat or drink because he was so upset and sad at all the horrible things he had done to people who followed Jesus. Saul had done those things because he really believed Jesus was not the Promised One, and now he knew the truth. His hard heart was softening, but as it softened, it was also getting sad.

At the same time Saul was blind and not eating or drinking anything, God was preparing someone else to help Saul. God spoke to a man named Ananias and told him where to find Saul, who was praying. God wanted Ananias to pray over Saul to give him back his sight and then to help him begin following Jesus. Ananias was scared at first. He knew Saul had been killing followers of Jesus, but God told him He had big plans for Saul and he would tell people all over the world about Jesus.

So Ananias obeyed God and found Saul. When Ananias did as God commanded, Saul's eyes were fixed so he could see again. Ananias baptized him, and Saul began to eat and become strong again.

God kept His promise to Ananias about how He would use Saul. Later, God changed Saul's name to Paul, but it was this same man who went all over the world and told people about Jesus. He was put in prison for telling people about Jesus. He was beaten for telling people about Jesus. But he was also very faithful with a soft heart toward God, loving Jesus every day of the rest of his life and serving Him even when it hurt.

—FROM ACTS 9

Questions

* **What had Saul been doing at the beginning of the story?**
* **What happened to Saul while he was on the road?**
* **What did God ask Ananias to do?**
* **How would you have felt if you were Ananias and God asked you to go see Saul?**

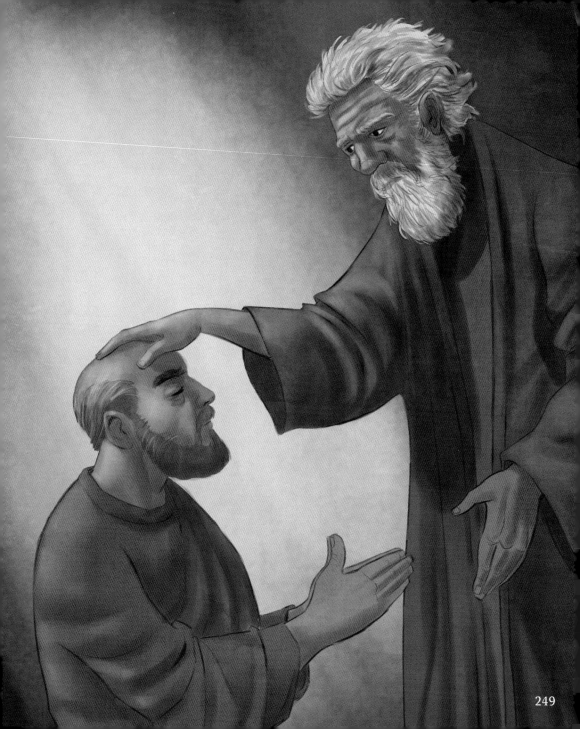

God's Promised Perfect Time

More and more people became followers of Jesus, and they began to meet together in the very first churches and do many of the things we do in church today. They would sing songs of praise to God, and they would hear teaching from what Jesus taught when He was on earth. They didn't have the Bible yet, so they would often hear from someone who had actually heard Jesus teach.

Paul went on many trips to new cities to tell people about Jesus and start new churches. When he started a new church, he would stay there for as long as he could and teach them. One of those first churches he started was in a town called Thessalonica. When it was time for Paul to go to the next city, he left them in the care of another teacher. But over time some new teachers came and started teaching the church things that weren't true and weren't what Jesus had taught.

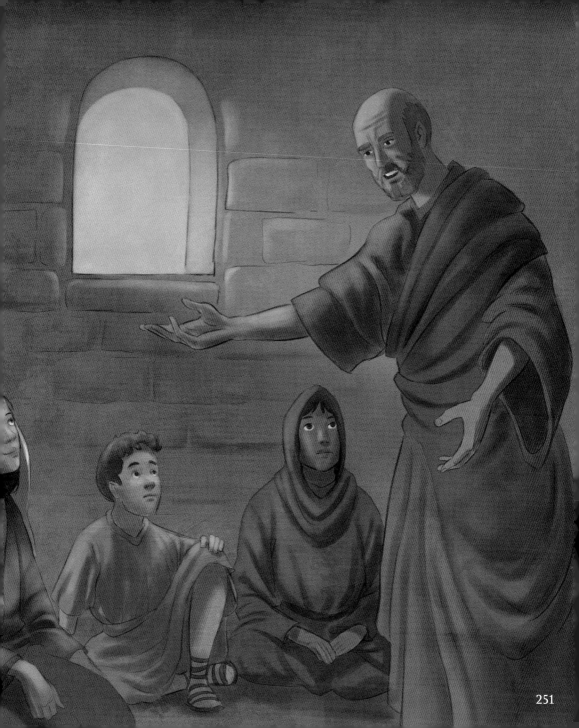

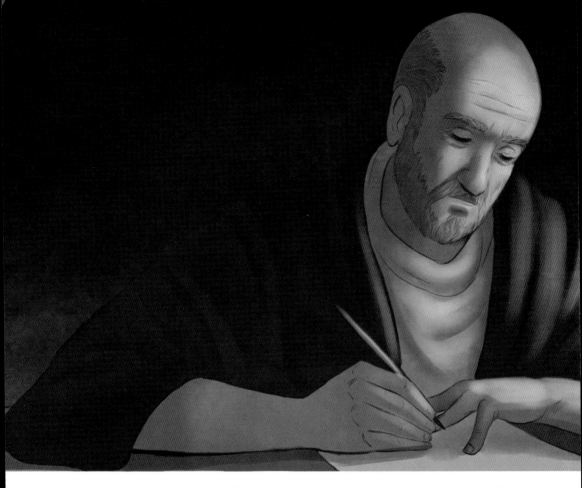

Paul heard about this and was very sad because he knew that the only way to follow Jesus is to know what is true. He couldn't go back to see the people in Thessalonica, but he could write a letter. He wrote them two letters that we have as part of the Bible today. These letters teach us today just like they taught the church in Thessalonica a very long time ago.

The people in Thessalonica were doing great in some ways. They loved Jesus and had soft hearts toward Him. But they had let bad teachers come in and teach them things that Paul had already taught them weren't true. One of the big things that these bad teachers were teaching was that Jesus had already

come back to earth again. Well, it was true that Jesus had promised that one day He would return and set up His kingdom on earth. But Jesus had said that only God the Father knew when that day would be, and Paul knew that it had not yet come.

Paul wrote these followers of Jesus and reminded them that only God knows the day Jesus will return. And when He does, everyone will know it, and we won't have to wonder. Paul assured the people that Jesus had not yet returned and encouraged them to keep doing the work they had been given to do.

We are waiting for Jesus to return too! While we wait, we need to do the work God has given us to do. For those of us who follow Jesus, part of our work is to tell other people about Jesus. For grown-ups, we may also have a job to work to take care of ourselves or our families. For children like you, your job is to learn and to obey your parents. Paul reminded people in Thessalonica that these jobs needed to be done while doing the work of telling others about Jesus. And we need these reminders today too.

Paul encouraged the followers of Jesus in Thessalonica. He reminded them again and again of how much he cared for them and how much hope they had in Jesus. He also challenged them to be really strong, to stand up for the things he had taught them from Jesus, and not to listen to anything else.

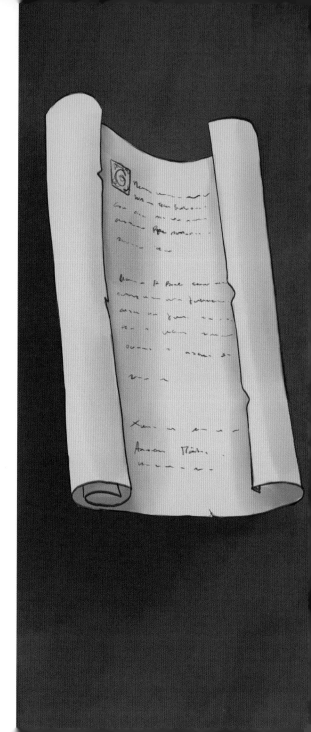

Paul wrote these letters to the church in Thessalonica thousands of years ago. But God put them in the Bible because they're also promises for us today, and they have been for followers of Jesus from the beginning. We are all to wait for Him to come back and not worry about when it will be, because God knows the perfect time. And we are to listen only to teachers who teach what matches the things Jesus taught. And we should encourage one another to work hard telling people about Jesus like Paul did!

—*FROM 1 & 2 THESSALONIANS*

Questions

* **Did Paul start one church or a lot of churches?**

* **How were these churches like our churches today?**

* **What was one of the things the church in Thessalonica was believing that was wrong?**

* **What was something Paul encouraged the church in Thessalonica to do that we can and should do today?**

Promised Gifts for All

Paul also started a church in a city called Corinth. This church had many problems after Paul left, and once again he had to write two letters to help the people, who were called the Corinthians.

Paul told the Corinthians two big things that can help us today too. First, he told them what love is and what it isn't, all to show us a picture of what a soft heart is and to remind us of how Jesus is. Paul said that love is patient, which means that when you love someone, you don't get angry really fast. He said that love doesn't brag or act better than other people. If we do, our hearts are not being soft and loving. We don't show love to make God pleased with us. We show love because we love God and want to be like Jesus, who loved people the very best that anyone has ever loved anyone ever!

Paul said that one thing love doesn't do is keep track of when someone does something wrong. So, if you get upset about something, it isn't loving to bring it back up to the person who upset you after they've apologized. That means Jesus doesn't keep track of our sins after we've asked for forgiveness; and that's a wonderful thing! Imagine if Jesus had a list of every single sin you had ever done and was keeping track and then when you prayed to Him, all He did was tell you how much you had upset Him with each of those sins. That wouldn't be like Jesus, would it? When we follow Him, we try to love like He loves, which means we don't keep lists of how people make us angry.

257

Another big thing Paul taught the Corinthians is a promise from God. Paul explained that God promises to give special gifts to every person who follows Jesus. Now these aren't like the kinds of gifts you unwrap on your birthday. These are spiritual gifts that are built inside of you. They're special things you can do that serve the church, like being a good singer, or teacher, or someone who loves to pray, or someone who happily serves other people. God's gifts could be lots of things.

The Corinthians were saying that some gifts were better than others and fighting over which were best. Paul said to stop fighting because all the spiritual gifts are the same to God, and all of them work together to make a whole church. The church is made up of women and men and boys and girls who have different personalities and gifts. Each of them is important to God and part of what makes the whole church work. It's sort of like a gigantic puzzle, and everyone who is a follower of Jesus is one of the pieces. Without your piece, it wouldn't be whole, and none of the pieces is more important than other pieces!

—FROM 1 & 2 CORINTHIANS

Questions

* Can you name one thing Paul said love is?
* Can you name one thing Paul said love isn't?
* What is a spiritual gift?
* Is one spiritual gift better than another?

259

The Freedom Promise

When Paul wrote letters to the churches, most of the time he was kind and gentle, telling them what they were doing wrong or how to live for God. But one church had Paul so confused, so amazed with how ridiculous the people were acting, that he had to speak to them very firmly to correct them. This church was in a town called Galatia.

Here's what was happening. Paul had gone to Galatia and taught the people there for quite a while. He taught them about how sin had separated us from God and had made our hearts hard toward Him. That meant there had to be a sacrifice for us to be reconnected to God and have hearts like His. Paul had taught the Galatians about how no matter how many good things we did, there was no way we could ever do enough to make up for the sin that is in us. We would have to be perfect, and we can't be perfect because of how Adam and Eve's sin changed their hearts and our hearts forever.

Except it didn't have to be forever.

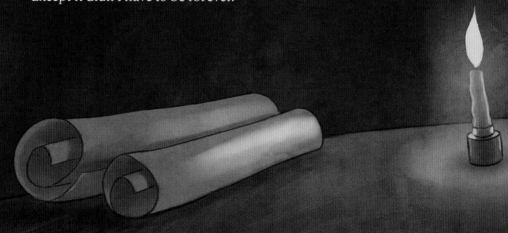

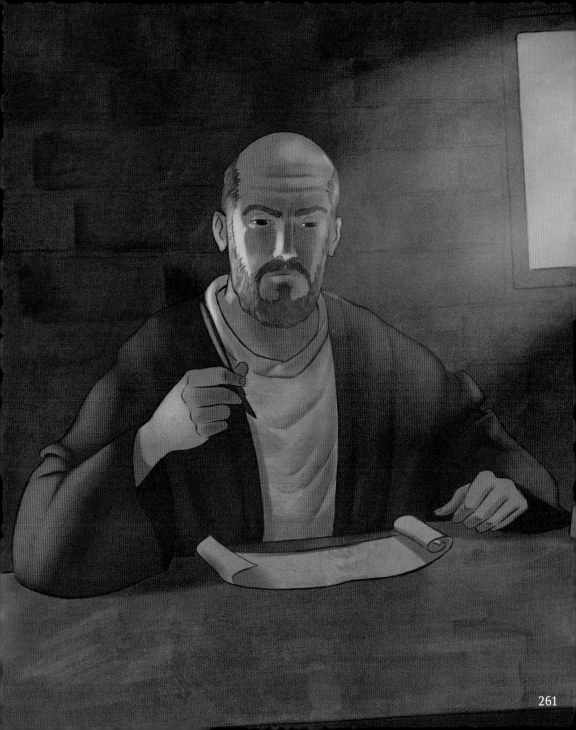

Paul had told the Galatians how Jesus was God who had come to earth to be with us and to fix this sin problem for us. The way He did this was by living a perfect life and never sinning. Jesus always obeyed His Father, which meant Jesus obeyed so much that He let Himself be put to death on a cross even when He had done nothing wrong.

Paul had explained to the Galatians that this was so important: because Jesus had never done anything wrong when He was put on the cross, God could put all the sins we *have* done on Jesus. But God didn't stop there. For everybody who trusts in Jesus, God puts on them the perfection of Jesus. This means that for everyone who trusts in Jesus, God doesn't see their sin, He sees Jesus's perfection! Jesus got the sin, and those who follow Him get His perfection, which means our hearts are made soft again. And since Jesus did not stay dead, but came back to life, if we believe in Him, we will one day come back to life like Him and get to be with God forever after our lives on this earth.

Paul had explained all this to the Galatians. The only thing they had to do for their sins to be forgiven and to receive the perfection of Jesus was to believe that Jesus was the Son of God, the One who died on the cross to pay for our sins but came back to life to show that He was God and had won over death.

Well, that all seems pretty clear, right?

The Galatians believed Paul, and they followed that way for a while. But then they started listening to the wrong voices (just like Eve had done!). They started believing they needed to do all the things Paul had told them PLUS other things before God could forgive their sins. They came up with all sorts of rules—some of the rules from long before Jesus came, which made it sound as if Jesus had never come or didn't do enough. This made Paul frustrated with the Galatians because he wanted them to believe the Truth so badly.

So Paul wrote the Galatians a letter. He reminded them that Jesus had given them freedom. If they added a bunch of new, made-up rules, they would be living like prisoners when Jesus wanted them to be free!

—*FROM GALATIANS*

Questions

* How was Paul feeling toward the Galatian church?
* What did Paul teach them was the way to have their sins forgiven?
* Is this any different from how we have our sins forgiven?
* Have you told Jesus you believe in Him and asked Him to be the One—the only One—to forgive you of your sins?

265

The Promise and Providence of Love

Paul's longest letter was to the church in Rome. It was also the only letter he wrote to a church he had not yet visited. He wasn't writing them because they were doing anything wrong. He just wanted to encourage them with the Truth and help them stay faithful to Jesus.

Paul told the Romans that God had kept the promise He made in the garden, the promise to send One who would defeat death—Jesus! Paul told them, just like he did the Galatians, that trusting Jesus was the only way to be saved from our sin and have our hearts reconnected to God.

Paul said that it didn't matter if the whole world was against us as long as God was for us—that's how important following Jesus is.

At first Paul wrote how the Romans had to believe in Jesus and trust only Him to be saved. But then he began to write about what is true for those who are followers of Jesus and what God's love is like for those who love Jesus and follow Him.

ROME

For those who follow Jesus, Paul said, nothing can ever separate them from the love of God. That is a big and wonderful promise for God to make. It means that if you are a follower of Jesus, you can never mess up so bad that God will love you any less. And it means that if you are a follower of Jesus, no one else can ever do anything to you that will make God love you any less.

But that wasn't the only promise God made in Paul's letter to the Romans. Paul also told them that no matter what happens to someone who is a follower of Jesus, God will always make it work out so that it is good. This means that even when things look like they are horrible, they won't stay horrible if you love and follow Jesus, because God has a plan to show everyone how good a God He is and how much He cares for us.

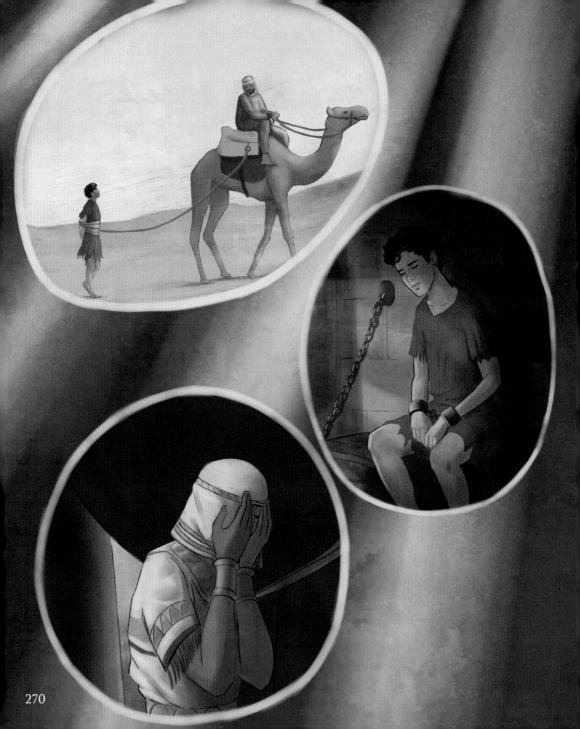

270

Remember when we learned about Joseph? Joseph lived long before Jesus lived, but Joseph had a heart that loved God, and he believed that God was sending the One who would save them some day. Well, remember how Joseph's brothers sold him into slavery? That was a bad thing that happened to Joseph, but Joseph didn't stay a slave. No, he ended up being one of the king's helpers so that Egypt was able to save food for all the people, including Joseph's family.

Joseph had to wait many, many years before he saw his brothers or his father again. Those long years could have seemed like nothing more than a horrible thing because he missed his family so much. But the Bible says that when Joseph did see his brothers, he forgave them and told them that God had always planned for this to be how things happened.

Joseph's story is exactly like what Paul was writing to the Romans about. And those stories don't just happen to people in the Bible, they happen to people like us all the time. Sometimes things can seem impossible, and life may truly be very sad and difficult; but if we love and follow Jesus, God will one day make all that pain and sadness go away and everything make sense. Just like God promised, He loves us so much that nothing can take us away from His love!

—*FROM ROMANS*

Questions

* Had Paul ever visited the church in Rome?

* Paul told the Romans about two big promises from God in this letter. Can you remember what the one was about love?

* Can you remember what the promise was about things that happen to us?

* What is something that has happened to you that has been sad or made you upset that you wish God would fix and make better?

271

Chosen with the Promise of Spiritual Armor

Paul also wrote a letter to the church in the city of Ephesus. The people were doing the things they had been taught, so Paul wanted to encourage them. This letter is a good example of writing someone just to say "good job" and not waiting until they do something wrong. What's so amazing is that Paul was writing to encourage the Ephesians and remind them of the promises of God while he was in prison! He had been taken prisoner for preaching about Jesus.

Paul reminded the Ephesians of two of God's main promises for those who follow Jesus. First, they had been chosen by God to follow Jesus from before the world was even made! That's right—before God even made the light and the dark, He chose everyone who would ever follow Jesus. Now He didn't choose them because of anything special about them, because compared to Jesus everyone is just a sinner who can't do anything good without God. But instead, God chose them because He knew what would make it most clear that He is the only God, the One who is good and powerful and should be worshiped. Paul explained that because God had chosen the followers of Jesus long ago, God promises that each of them will one day get to be with Jesus as He is made King forever.

Second, Paul knew that living in this world is difficult because we still have hearts that get hard and sin. Followers of Jesus can always ask Him to forgive them and receive that forgiveness, but we need to do more than that to try to fight sin. We need to say no to the enemy and instead say yes to God. Paul said it's like being in a war! That's how serious it is. It's not a war against people. It's a war against Satan and the bad things in this world that want us to disobey God. Well, we all know that soldiers don't go to war dressed in their normal clothes or without weapons! They go to war wearing armor, and Paul said God has promised to give those who follow Jesus the armor they need to beat sin.

God promises that when we wear this armor, we will be able to stand against Satan and be obedient to God. The first piece of the armor is the belt of Truth, which means that we are to be surrounded and held up by what God has said. This was Adam and Eve's first mistake in the garden—they did not listen to and obey what God had said was true. The belt of Truth will keep us surrounded and held up by Truth.

The second piece of armor is the breastplate of righteousness. Righteousness means that we will make wise decisions that show hearts that are soft like God's. The breastplate covers the heart and protects it as we make these decisions. The third piece of armor is the shoes for our feet, shoes we wear as we go and share the good news of Jesus and the peace He brings. The next piece of armor we need is the shield of faith, which helps us remember what Jesus has done and believe in His power to overcome our enemies.

Then we are to put on the helmet of salvation, which protects our minds from believing things that aren't true about Jesus and how we are saved. Then, finally, we are to hold the sword of the Spirit, which is the Bible. By knowing God's words (which is what the Bible is), we can defeat our enemies with His words.

Paul said that with this spiritual armor, we will be able to defeat the enemy and stand strong no matter what. God promises to give this armor to all those who follow Jesus so that we can be prepared to always be faithful to Him!

—*FROM EPHESIANS*

Questions

* **When did God choose all those who would follow Jesus?**
* **Why did God choose those who follow Jesus?**
* **Can you name the pieces of spiritual armor God promises to give all those who follow Jesus?**
* **What piece of armor do you think is most important?**

The Complete Promise

Paul was still in prison when he wrote to a church that was made up of some of his best friends and helpers. The church in the town of Philippi had been the first one to really love and support Paul while he traveled to tell people about Jesus and start new churches. He knew those people (the Philippians) had heard he was in prison and were worried about him, so he wrote a letter to encourage them and to remind them of God's Truth.

The letter to the Philippians contains one of the most hopeful and biggest promises from God in the whole Bible: God will finish doing all the good things He has started doing with His people. This being in the Bible means it is a promise for everyone who follows Jesus. We can trust that when God starts doing something, He will always finish it. He will never ever leave us or forget about us. We can never be so far away that He can't find us or so quiet that He can't hear us. And for those who follow Jesus, even if we sin and try to turn from God, He will always come for us, find us, and lead us back to Him. He has a plan for everyone's life, and when someone follows Jesus, he or she gets the promise that God will always finish that plan.

This is amazing news because a lot of times in life we are sad by things that don't go how we expect them to go. We may be excited about going to a birthday party but then get sick and can't go. Or we may hope to have a baby brother or sister, but God never gives us one. Well, even though those kinds of disappointing things happen in our lives, if we are followers of Jesus, then we know God does have plans for every single day of our lives, and those plans will always be finished. He will never ever forget about us or give up on us.

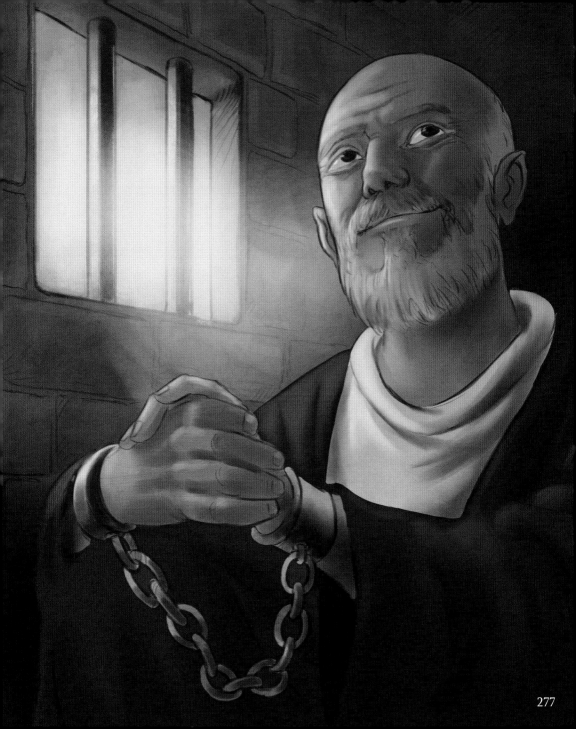

But Paul didn't share only that one promise from God with the Philippians. He also told them lots of other things that made them feel hopeful, and those things are important for us to remember too. He told them to remember that as followers of Jesus, they needed to have hearts like Him. Jesus is God, and because He is God, He could have commanded angels to come and get Him off the cross. He could have destroyed those men who were crucifying Him. But that isn't what Jesus did. Instead, He thought of us. He thought of others as more important than Himself even though no one ever will be more important than Jesus!

Paul told the Philippians this is how they should treat each other too. Instead of thinking about what they wanted and what was best for them, they should think about what others wanted instead. They shouldn't pout or complain . . . because Jesus definitely didn't pout or complain.

The day was coming, Paul said, when Jesus will return and everyone who has ever lived will bow before Him and call to Him as God. Everyone, even those who crucified Him, will know that He really was who He said He was, and they will know that Jesus will reign over the new world He is creating!

—*FROM PHILIPPIANS*

Questions

* **Where was Paul when he wrote to the Philippians?**
* **What did Paul promise God will do when He begins something for His people?**
* **What did Paul tell them about how Jesus acted when He was being crucified?**
* **How did Paul want the Philippians to treat each other?**

Promised New Life

Paul wrote to another church that was having problems with bad teaching. He had to remind them of Truth about God and how they should follow Him. This church was in a town called Colossae.

The people in Colossae were called Colossians, and Paul reminded them of a very important promise for all those who follow Jesus. Jesus is more important than anything else in the whole universe, and everything is held together because of Jesus. He is the One we will worship for all time because He is the Promised One.

Paul reminded the Colossians that because they had chosen to follow Jesus, they were supposed to walk with Him. If you walk with someone, that means you go in the same direction and end up in the same place. So if we walk with Jesus, we will end up where Jesus wants us to be, and we will be doing what Jesus wants us to be doing. As we walk with Him more and more, we will become more and more like Him. When babies are learning to walk, they fall down a lot, but as they try again and again, they eventually walk without falling down. This is how it is for those who follow Jesus. We will get stronger in Him as we walk with Him and learn more about Him.

281

Paul went on and shared a really amazing promise from God. Remember how Jesus didn't stay dead? He was dead, but then He came back to life. Now, when He came back to life, He didn't stay on earth. He went to heaven to be with His Father. But Jesus definitely stayed alive and is still alive today. Well, Paul told the Colossians that for all of us who were stuck like dead people in our sin and unable to do anything except sin, when we believed and followed Jesus, God made a huge change in us. Instead of us being dead and stuck dying, He made it so that we are like Jesus. That means that even when we die on this earth, God promises that we will stay alive like Jesus, which means we will one day go and live with God just like Jesus did!

Paul hoped that all this encouragement would remind the Colossians to love and worship Jesus more. And we can do the same! If we are following Jesus and walking with Jesus, then being reminded of God's promises will make us want to worship Him more and walk with Him more closely.

God makes us promises so that we can love, hear, and obey Him, and we obey Him by following Jesus. Then God forgives all our sins and makes it so that we will be together with Jesus and alive forever. This should make us all love Jesus so much! If He hadn't died on the cross for the sins of all those who believe in Him, then none of this would be possible. We would be stuck in our sins. But we aren't stuck. We have hope. And Paul told the Colossians that hope is Jesus!

— FROM COLOSSIANS

Questions

* Why was Paul writing to the church in Colossae?
* What was the promise that God told the church in Colossae about what happens to followers of Jesus after they die?
* What happens if we walk with someone? What happens if we walk with Jesus?
* Why does God give us these promises?

Promise for the Nations

So far, all the things we've read from the Bible are things that already happened in the past. But now we are going to have some stories that are about things that haven't happened yet. It's a lot like when the prophets long ago were telling people about Jesus before Jesus had come. Only this time, God told one of the disciples, John, a bunch of things about what God is going to do one day in the future. God told John to write it down so it could be in the Bible. It's in the Bible's very last book, Revelation, and we're going to have three stories about three different promises from that book. All of them are things that haven't happened yet but are going to happen one day.

To understand the first promise we're going to talk about, we need to remember waaaaaaayyyyy back to the beginning when we learned about the promise God made to Abraham. Remember how God promised Abraham that one day He would make a whole huge group of people to be God's people and how they would all come from Abraham's family? Well, Jesus came from Abraham's family. And from Jesus, God made it so that all the people in the whole world could become followers of Jesus.

In fact, God gave John a picture in his mind of what heaven is going to look like one day. And when He did, He made sure John knew that this wasn't just an idea or something John was imagining; it was a promise. It will happen. In this picture, John saw more people than anyone could count. But they weren't people who looked alike. They were people with all different colors of skin. All different kinds of hair. All different colored eyes. All different heights. All different shapes. All different languages. From all different countries.

Except not everything was different about them.

Some things were the same.

They were all wearing white robes.

And they all had palm branches in their hands.

And most importantly, they were all standing around the throne that Jesus was sitting on, and they were shouting, "Salvation belongs to our God who is seated on the throne!"

These people were in heaven, alive with Christ, just like God had promised the Colossians. The people were all shouting that they had been saved from their sins because of Jesus, who is God and who was sitting on the throne. That's a lot of the promises we've learned about all together in one!

But this picture of heaven also has a new promise in it. When all of us who follow Jesus meet together to worship Him in heaven, we will get to do so with people from all over the world who also love Jesus and know He is the only way for their sins to be forgiven. God promises us that He will save people from all over the whole world, not just from where we live and not just people who look or talk like us!

—*FROM REVELATION 7*

Questions

* **What did God give John to write about?**

* **Have these things already happened, or are they things that are still going to happen?**

* **What did God promise Abraham He would do for him?**

* **What did John see that God told him was a promise of how it was going to be?**

Promising All Things New

God continued to give John a picture of what God will do in the future. He showed John how Satan would be fully destroyed, just as God promised in the garden. He showed John how Jesus would arrive on a white horse, riding victoriously. And then He showed John a new picture of something incredible . . . an amazing promise for us to enjoy.

He showed John a new heaven, a new earth, a new Jerusalem (which was where God's temple had been), and a river of life. These were not like the heaven and earth and Jerusalem or rivers we have today. The ones we have today are the way they are because of sin and brokenness. Flowers die. People are sad. Rivers dry up. Bones break. People die. All sorts of bad things happen that make us feel sad or angry. And worst of all, we sin on this earth.

But all those things that are part of this world will be gone when God sends the new creation. The new world will be perfect. Nothing will ever die, and no one will ever cry. God showed John that not only will this world be perfect, but God will also live with us there! We will be with Him just like Adam and Eve were with Him in the garden before they sinned!

Then God had an angel take John up to a tall mountain to show him a picture of the new Jerusalem, a perfect and beautiful place for us to worship God. Its walls will be made of shiny jewels, and its streets will be made of pure gold. It won't even need to have the sun or moon shining on it because God's presence will light it so that it is always light. Close your eyes for just a second and imagine what this might look like.

But there was even more to see. The angel showed John the river of life, which was bright like crystal and flowed all through the city to the tree of life. All through the year, this special tree was filled with twelve different kinds of fruit.

God allowed John to see such truly incredible sights. We are used to the parts of our world that are bad and broken because of sin, but nearly everything in our world is different than it will be in the new earth. There will be no sin there. Everyone who has followed Jesus will be there, with hearts that are perfectly connected to His. We will love, hear, and obey Him always.

God could have left us on this earth forever, but He is a loving God with a plan and promises. He knew we would disobey Him in the garden. He knew Jesus would have to save us from sin. He knew we would keep struggling to obey Him as long as we are on this earth. So God always planned to show creation how wonderful He is by creating the new heaven, new earth, new Jerusalem, and the river of life for all the followers of Jesus!

—*FROM REVELATION 21–22*

Questions

✳ What did God do to Satan?

✳ What did God show John coming down from above?

✳ What are some things that won't be in the new earth?

✳ Who will Jesus's followers live with in the new earth?

The Promised Return and Rule

God showed John one final picture of what was going to happen one day. This picture was the most remarkable of all. It was Jesus on the throne, being worshiped. But not only that, He was reigning. He was the King that He was always intended to be. All those on the new earth were loving and worshiping Him, so God showed John that one day His people will rule right alongside Jesus.

That's right, these are the same people who once lived on this broken earth and sinned and had hard hearts toward God. Then they turned away from their sin and turned toward Jesus, trusting Him to save them. God promises that one day in the future, they will be made perfect and be in the new earth with Jesus, ruling alongside Him. That is a promise for everyone who follows Jesus. Every single person, those who were children when they started following Jesus and those who were grown-ups . . . they all get to be with Him.

Isn't this the most incredible promise of all!?!

All those who follow Jesus will have everything that Adam and Eve had in the garden, only more. We will know that God has suffered for us, that He loves us deeply, and we will know that He is the only way to have any hope. We will worship Him with our whole hearts because we will know that without Him our hearts would be hardened and unable to hear, love, or worship Him.

We will be thankful.

We will be free.

We will be with Jesus.

294

And this could happen any day. It could happen tonight. Or tomorrow. Or next month. Or next year. We don't know when Jesus is coming back, but one of the last things God told John was that He IS coming. He told John that He is coming soon and that until He comes, we should obey all the words in the Bible.

So that is what we are trying to do. We have been learning about the promises of God so we will know that God is the One who works in our lives to change us. We cannot do enough to be good for God. We cannot make promises to God that save us. *His* promises to us are what saves us, what gives us hope, and what helps us know how to follow Him.

And all of those promises are because God loves Jesus, He loves you, and He wants you to know and love Jesus. He created you, and He knows every single day of your life. He knows every hair on your head, and no one in the whole entire world loves you as much as He does. Even these promises can't contain His love for you. So now, as we finish this book, we want to pray for the day when Jesus will come back. We can pray that it will be soon and that when He comes, we will all be ready. That He will find us all following Him and loving Him, ready to go and rule with Him!

Let's pray . . .

—*FROM REVELATION 22*

Words of Gratitude

*H*aving published hundreds of books and edited millions of words over the course of my publishing career, I never thought I would find myself on this side of the process. As I pray and trust that God will bring fruit from these pages, you certainly know that there are many people without whom this book of Bible stories would not be in your hands. I hope you read this and are introduced to some of them here.

I must first acknowledge and thank the best team in publishing. I've always known this as the leader of the team, but now I've gotten to experience it as an author. I'm especially thankful for Michelle (Burke) Freeman, who was able to guide this first-time author (who happened to be her boss) with all the skill, knowledge, and poise I've always seen in her. Michelle, you are incomparably gifted at your work, and I am deeply grateful for this opportunity to work with you. Distinct gratitude also goes out to Rachel Shaver, Diana Lawrence, and Kristi Smith for their respective marketing and design skills that join together so that people will pick this book up and buy it. They, too, have been able to see this message for what it is and what it can be in the lives of families, rather than being distracted by my role as the boss. This was one of my greatest concerns, but they, along with the leadership of Devin Maddox (who shoulders for the team everything that can't fit on my shoulders), have made me both grateful and proud to work alongside them.

Along with my publishing team, this book would not be the beautiful book it is without the giftedness of Thanos Tsilis. Thank you so much, Thanos, for pouring so much into this so quickly and for being patient with an author with a very specific vision. You have brought my imagination to life, and I am deeply grateful.

My teaching is grounded in the education and discipleship I have been blessed to receive. The Southern Baptist Theological Seminary didn't just grant me a degree, it discipled me and provided the foundation necessary for me to teach God's Word to others. I've also been blessed by a group of seven older women who have walked with me for more than ten years now, modeling what ministry faithfulness looks like amidst life's trials and Satan's schemes. They have encouraged me to be the godliest version of myself and have been patient with this "baby" of the group who so often wears that label fully—despite my age or what I should be. They have encouraged me as I worked on this project and carried me in prayer through difficult days that hit in the middle of it. They are my beloved sisters who have taught and discipled me through their consistent, faithful love and witnesses. I love you all so much and praise God for you.

There are countless other friends who have supported me in many ways as I've completed this work, who have been more patient with me than I deserve, and more understanding than I can imagine, and whom I'm not naming lest I inadvertently leave someone out. But if you get texts from me at all hours of the night, you know that you are one of these friends!

There is one single individual, though, whom I would be remiss not to acknowledge as having a strong role shaping the framework for the heart behind this book, as well as sustaining me in a multitude of ways as I wrote. Mary Anne Severino, otherwise known as the best therapist on earth, I remember the first time you talked to me about my heart. I remember cringing, while staring at your heart paperweight, and being afraid of conversations about hearts because I thought mine was so bad.

Over the last few years, you have shown me things about the heart and God's heart for us that I had never even imagined. This has defined much of what I teach my Sunday School class each week and is a thread throughout this book. You will never know how your care, patience, and giftedness helped shape this book while also being used by God to shape me into someone who could write it. Words will never suffice, but thankfully, you know my heart. And you know it is full of gratitude to you and to God who led me to you.

The significant role that Grace Community Church of Nashville has played in my life for the past ten years cannot be overstated. God has used that congregation, each week's sermon, and my opportunity to teach the three-year-old kiddos there to nurture and sustain my faith through challenges great and small. Scott and Beth Patty have walked with me through times when it seemed a project like this would never be possible, always encouraging me toward the steadfastness of the Lord. Jason Miller has been the world's most patient children's pastor who has given me a ministry home within the church . . . even when I often want to do things my own way for the specific children I'm teaching. And, to the parents of Grace, tears come to my eyes as I write my thanks to you. Thank you for letting me teach your three-year-old children each week. Thank you for bringing them to GCC to learn about God. I'm praying with you that God will grant each of them soft hearts that hear, love, and obey Him.

This book is dedicated in part to the loving memory of Job Wilson Kemp. Job was a little three-year-old when I first met him. Quiet at first, but with the ability to turn to a fit of giggles pretty much at warp speed. I have many memories of the year I got to teach Job, watching him grow into a more confident four-year-old, but none stand out as much as when he pressed me to explain the Trinity (asking me, of course, in a four-year-old's words). This was a new question, and he pressed in with many follow-up questions, trying to understand fully what is incomprehensible to most adults. I did my best to explain, not knowing that just over a year later, he would be in the presence of our mysterious, loving, faithful God whom I tried to explain that day. My heart never ceases to be broken for the loss his parents, siblings, and very large, loving extended family have experienced. For the loss our church experienced. And for the loss I experienced not getting to see him grow up within our church. For many months, God had impressed upon me to write this book, but it was only at Job's memorial service, as his dad proclaimed Psalm 103, that I relinquished my fears and surrendered. I did so because I believe we can never assume how long we will have to teach someone about the promises of God and how they are fulfilled to His people in Christ. So, to Chase and Katie Kemp, especially, thank you for letting me teach your precious son and for allowing me to remember Job through every page of this book.

Finally, it is traditional to either start or end the acknowledgments with a word of thanks to God. Indeed, there are a multitude of means and reasons why this book would not be possible apart from Him, His grace in my life, and His steadfast love. But the beauty is that I don't need to type it for God to know it. So, instead, I simply thank Him for His ability to know my heart and the depths of my desperation and gratitude for Him. Immanuel.

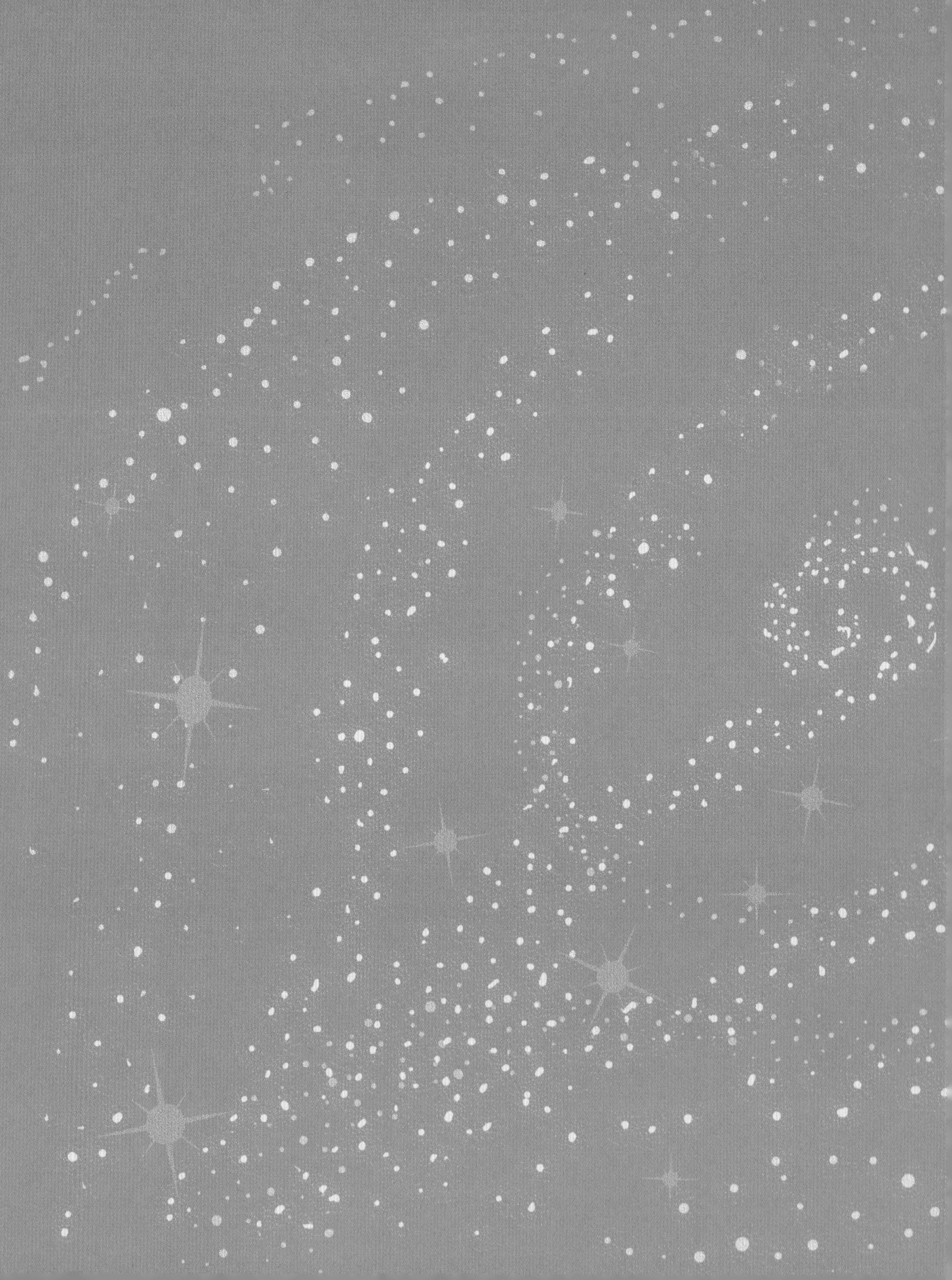

About the Author

JENNIFER LYELL has had the honor of teaching the Bible to women, teens, and children of all ages, in both the United States and overseas. While she is grateful to open God's Word anytime she's given the opportunity, teaching children eclipses it all and is the most enriching and joy-filled experience in her life. Jennifer considers teaching and discipleship her primary calling from God, but a love for books and the written word has permeated her life since she was a small child. Her passion for biblically faithful and personally engaging children's books runs deep.

In addition to her teaching ministry, Jennifer served for more than a decade as book publisher for LifeWay Christian Resources. The hundreds of titles that the book publishing team acquired, developed, or managed under Jennifer's leadership included more than a dozen *New York Times* bestsellers, as well as multiple *Christianity Today* Book of the Year winners. Jennifer holds a Master of Divinity Degree from The Southern Baptist Theological Seminary, which is good because she has been asked questions by preschoolers that she wouldn't have been able to answer without it! Jennifer is often an off-the-path hiker who is always happy when adventuring (just like a child!).